The BIG BOOK of LOGOS 3

David E. Carter
Editor

The Big Book of Logos 3

First published in 2002 by HBI,
an imprint of HarperCollins Publishers
10 East 53rd Street
New York, NY 10022-5299

Distributed in the U.S. and Canada by
Watson-Guptill Publications
770 Broadway
New York, NY 10003-9595
Tel: (800) 451-1741
          (732) 363-4511 in NJ, AK, HI
Fax: (732) 363-0338

ISBN: 0-8230-0539-9

Distributed throughout the rest of the world by
HarperCollins International
10 East 53rd Street
New York, NY 10022-5299
Fax: (212) 207-7654

ISBN: 0-06-620940-4

Printed in Hong Kong by Everbest Printing Company through Four
Colour Imports, Louisville, Kentucky.

Book and jacket design by *Designs on You!*.

By gosh, we've done it again.

First, there was **The Big Book of Logos**. It became a big seller. Actually it became a huge seller.

And so, there was a demand for **The NEW Big Book of Logos**. Same thing. Designers from all over the world discovered that those two books are a great source of inspiration and ideas for logo design.

So they all said: "do it again."

This new **Big Book of Logos**, like the previous two, includes about 2,500 logos, all in full color. And if you design logos, this book (and the other two) really should be at your fingertips.

Why? So you can see what's happening out there in the big world of logo design. There's no larger source than this book (and the other two), and there's no more up-to-date source on logo design than **The Big of Logos 3**.

1.

2.

freerein

3.

BrainShare2000

4.

5.

6.

bucky®

7.

APTIMUS

8.

4

impli

9.

HEAVENLY STONE

10.

11.

12.

maveron

13.

14.

(all)
Design Firm **Hornall Anderson Design Works**

1.
Client — *Care Future*
Designers — John Hornall, Jana Wilson Esser, Hillary Radbill, Sonja Max, Michael Brugman

2.
Client — *Seattle Convention & Visitors Bureau*
Designers — Jack Anderson, Lisa Cerveny, Gretchen Cook, Mary Hermes, Michael Brugman, Naomi Davidson, Hillary Radbill, Taka Sakita, Bruce Branson-Meyer, Mark Popich, Don Stayner, Mary Chin Hutchison

3.
Client — *Freerein*
Designers — Jack Anderson, Mark Popich, Tobi Brown, John Anicker, Steffanie Lorig, Bruce Stigler, Ensi Mofasser, Elmer Dela Cruz, John Anderle, Gretchen Cook

4.
Client — *Novell, Inc.*
Designers — Jack Anderson, Larry Anderson, Belinda Bowling, Michael Brugman

5.
Client — *Cougar Mountain Cookies*
Designers — Jack Anderson, Debra McCloskey, Lisa Cerveny, Mary Chin Hutchison, Gretchen Cook, Holly Craven, Dorothee Soechting

6.
Client — *GGLO*
Designers — Debra McCloskey, Steffanie Lorig, Ensi Mofasser, Tobi Brown

7.
Client — *Bucky*
Designers — Jack Anderson, Mary Hermes, Henry Yiu, Gretchen Cook, Elmer Dela Cruz

8.
Client — *Aptimus*
Designers — Jack Anderson, Katha Dalton, Bruce Branson-Meyer, Michael Brugman, Tobi Brown, Mary Hermes, Ed Lee

9.
Client — *Impli*
Designers — Jack Anderson, Kathy Saito, Sonja Max, Alan Copeland

10.
Client — *Heavenly Stone*
Designers — Jack Anderson, Henry Yiu

11.
Client — *etrieve*
Designers — John Hornall, Kathy Saito, Henry Yiu, Alan Copeland, Andrew Smith

12.
Client — *TruckBay*
Designers — Jack Anderson, Debra McCloskey, John Anderle, Andrew Wicklund

13.
Client — *Maveron*
Designers — Jack Anderson, Margaret Long

14.
Client — *CHOC (Children's Hospital of Orange County)*
Designers — Jack Anderson, Lisa Cerveny, Debra McCloskey, Jana Wilson Esser, Jana Nishi, Gretchen Cook, Steffanie Lorig

1.

2.

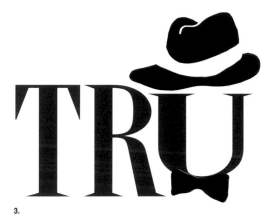

3.

4.

5.

6.

7.

8.

9.

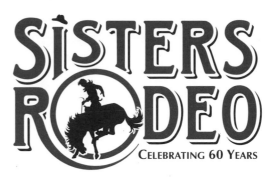

CELEBRATING 60 YEARS

10.

11.

12.

RONDONE◆KEMP
CAREER COUNSEL

14.

13.

15.

(all)
Design Firm **Jeff Fisher LogoMotives**
Designer Jeff Fisher

1.
Client *Sam Forencich/SamEyeAm*
Designer Jeff Fisher

2.
Client *Balloons on Broadway*
Designer Jeff Fisher

3.
Client *Triangle Productions!*
Designer Jeff Fisher

4.
Client *Black Dog Furniture Design*
Designer Jeff Fisher
Illustrator Brett Bigham

5.
Client *Rose City Softball Association*

6.
Client *DesignEire*
Designers Jeff Fisher, Nikita Jones

7.
Client *DataDork*
Designer Jeff Fisher

8.
Client *New England Firewood Company*
Designer Jeff Fisher

9.
Client *Lisa Horne & Family*
Designer Jeff Fisher

10.
Client *Sisters Rodeo Association*
Designers Jeff Fisher, Eloise Boren,
Sue Fisher (Triad)

11.
Client *Rose City Softball Association*
Designer Jeff Fisher

12.
Client *Portland Fire*
Designer Jeff Fisher, Brenda Jacobs

13.
Client *Page Six*
Designer Jeff Fisher

14.
Client *Rondone Kemp*
Designer Jeff Fisher

15.
Client *Triangle Productions!*
Designer Jeff Fisher

1.

2.

3.

4.

5.

6.

7.

8.

9.

10.

11.

12.

13.

14.

Portsmouth Vision 20/20

15.

1.

2.

3.

4.

5.

6.

7.

1 - 7

Design Firm **Graco Advertising**

1.
Client *Graco Industrial Division*
Designers Gary Schmidt, Karen Mefford

2.
Client *United Way—Internal*
Designer Gary Schmidt

3.
Client *4 Season Fun Club*
Designer Gloria Sheehan

4.
Client *Graco CED Division*
Designers David Orwoll, Bob Millard

5.
Client *Graco Industrial Division*
Designer Karen Mefford

6.
Client *Graco CED Division*
Designer David Orwoll

7.
Client *Graco Industrial Division*
Designer Gary Schmidt

opposite

Design Firm **Hornall Anderson Design Works**
Client *Bogart Golf*
Designers Jack Anderson, James Tee,
     Henry Yiu, Holly Craven,
     Mary Chin Hutchison

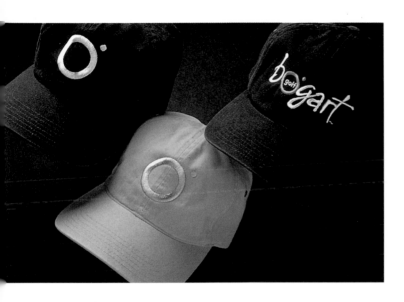

1.

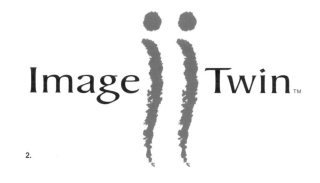

2.

3.

The Ridgefield Community Foundation

4.

MortgageSight

5.

S·T·S

6.

7.

La Jofferie™

8.

OceanConnect.com

9.

10.

11.

12.

DYNAPAC PHOTO

Professional Photo Lab

13.

14.

CaringAngels

assisted · living · services

15.

1, 11 - 13, 15
Design Firm **Dynapac Design Group**
2, 4 - 7, 9, 10, 14
Design Firm **Congdon and Company LLC**
3
Design Firm **Graphx Design Seattle**
8
Design Firm **Finished Art, Inc.**

1.
| Client | *Exotic Adventures* |
| Designer | Lee A. Aellig |

2.
| Client | *Image Twin* |
| Designers | Nathaniel Brockmann, Arthur Congdon |

3.
| Client | *Gallo Imports & Exports* |
| Designers | Valerie Forsythe, Patrick Smith, Anna Smith |

4.
| Client | *Ridgefield Community Foundation* |
| Designer | Arthur Congdon |

5.
| Client | *Mortgage Sight* |
| Designer | Nathaniel Brockmann |

6.
| Client | *STS Jewels* |
| Designer | Arthur Congdon |

7.
| Client | *Pepsi Cola* |
| Designer | Nathaniel Brockmann |

8.
| Client | *La Tofferie* |
| Designer | Kannex Fung |

9.
| Client | *Ocean Connect* |
| Designers | Nathaniel Brockmann, Arthur Congdon |

10.
| Client | *Pepsi Cola* |
| Designer | Nathaniel Brockmann |

11.
| Client | *ZCOR Incorporated* |
| Designer | Lee A. Aellig |

12.
| Client | *Lisa Valenzuela Vocal Cords Unlimited* |
| Designer | Lee A. Aellig |

13.
| Client | *Dynapac Photo* |
| Designer | Lee A. Aellig |

14.
| Client | *State of Florida* |
| Designer | Arthur Congdon |

15.
| Client | *Caring Angels* |
| Designer | Lee A. Aellig |

1.

2.

3.

4.

PLAZA
EAST
Office
Center

5.

Westport™

6.

7.

1 - 7
Design Firm **H2D Incorporated**
1.
Client   *M²*
Designers Joseph Hausch, Allan Haas
2.
Client   *Outward Focus*
Designers Joseph Hausch, Terry Lutz
3.
Client   *Johnson Wax*
Designers Joseph Hausch, Allan Haas
4.
Client   *Vigilo*
Designers Joseph Hausch, Jennifer Peck
5.
Client   *Plaza East*
Designers Joseph Hausch, Jennifer Peck
6.
Client   *Bemis Manufacturing*
Designers Allan Haas, Stacy Slutzky
7.
Client   *Consolidated Aviation*
Designers Joseph Hausch, Allan Haas,
              Terry Lutz

opposite
Design Firm **1-earth Graphics**
Client   *City of Piqua*
Designer Lisa Harris

1.

2.

3.

4.

5.

6.

7.

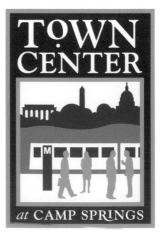

8.

من كن الغريين
AL GHURAIR CENTRE

9.

10.

11.

12.

Washingtonian Center

14.

13.

VICTORIA
GARDENS

15.

1, 3, 5 - 10, 13, 14
Design Firm **ID8/RTKL Associates Inc.**
2, 4, 11, 12, 15
Design Firm **Redmond Schwartz Design**

1.
Client ISLE of CAPRI
Designers Thom McKay, Jill Popowich

2.
Client Terra Mall
Designer Cody Clark

3.
Client Seoul Express
Terminal Co., LTD.
Designers Philips Engelke, Mi Kyung Lee

4.
Client Erini Redmond
Designer Suzanne Schwartz

5.
Client Sonae Imobiliaria SGPS, SA
Designers Phil Engelke, Jill Popowich

6.
Client CDR Associates
Designers Thom McKay, Mi Kyung Lee

7.
Client Centros Del Caribe S.A.
Designers Phil Engelke, Jill Popowich,
Ann Marie Verbrugge

8.
Client The Peter Schwartz Foundation
Designers Phil Engelke, Jill Popowich,
Lynne Barnard

9.
Client AL Ghurair Center
Designers Phil Engelke, Jill Popowich

10.
Client Mitsui Corporation
Designers Phil Engelke, Jill Popowich

11.
Client The Shops at Tanasbourne
Designers D. J. Thomas, Suzanne Schwartz

12.
Client Flatiron Marketplace
Designer Zuzana Jerieova

13.
Client Old Mutual Properties
Designers Greg Rose, Young Choe,
Phillips Engelke

14.
Client The Peterson Companies, LC
Designers Phil Engelke, Cindy Reppert,
Jill Popowich

15.
Client Victoria Gardens
Designer D. J. Thomas

17

1.

2.

3.

4.

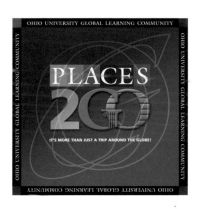

5.

6.

7.

8.

SPEAKEASY
C A S I N O

9.

DERBY™

28th RUNNING
August 12, 2000

10.

M A R B L E   T E C H N O L O G I E S ,   I N C .

11.

MTR GAMING GROUP, INC.

12.

SPEEDWAY
CASINO
LAS VEGAS

13.

P R E S Q U E   I S L E   D O W N S

14.

LA BONNE VIE
GOURMET RESTAURANT

15.

1 - 8
Design Firm **Ohio University**
9 - 15
Design Firm **Vance Wright Adams and Associates**

1.
Client — *Ohio University*
Designer — Mark Krumel

2.
Client — *Ohio University*
Designers — Mary Dillon, Mark Krumel

3.
Client — *Ohio University*
Designers — Mary Dillon, Mark Krumel

4.
Client — *Ohio University*
Designer — Mark Krumel

5.
Client — *Ohio University*
Designer — Mark Krumel

6.
Client — *Ohio University*
Designers — Mary Dillon, Mark Krumel

7.
Client — *Ohio University*
Designers — Mary Dillon, Mark Krumel

8.
Client — *Ohio University*
Designer — Mark Krumel

9.
Client — *MTR Gaming Group, Inc.*
Designers — Vance Wright Adams and Associates

10.
Client — *Mountaineer Race Track & Gaming Resort*
Designers — Vance Wright Adams and Associates

11.
Client — *Marble Technologies, Inc.*
Designers — Vance Wright Adams and Associates

12 - 14.
Client — *MTR Gaming Group, Inc.*
Designers — Vance Wright Adams and Associates

15.
Client — *Mountaineer Race Track & Gaming Resort*
Designers — Vance Wright Adams and Associates

peace works™

1.

d**mc**²

2.

ROBERT KOCH INSTITUT

3.

ETHYLENE OXIDE · EO EG · ETHYLENE GLYCOL

4.

THE
MARY BAKER EDDY LIBRARY
FOR THE BETTERMENT OF HUMANITY™

5.

INDIANA
INTERIORS, LLC

6.

7.

1 - 3
   Design Firm **MetaDesign**
4, 6
   Design Firm **Parsons and Maxson Inc.**
5
   Design Firm **Krent / Paffett Associates, Inc.**
7
   Design Firm **Gianopoulos Design**
1.
   Client   *peace works*
   Designers Uli Mayes, Marion Barbulla,
              Daniela Hensel, Fabian Rotthe,
              Jurgen Hubes, Natrin Androschin
2.
   Client   *Robert Koch-Institute*
   Designers Marion Burbulla, Fabian Rotthe,
              Uli Mayes, Daniela Hensel,
              Jurgen Hubes
3.
   Client   *dmc²*
   Designers Erik Spiekesmann,
              Robert Paulmann

4.
   Client   *The Dow Chemical Company*
   Designer   Sean Caldwell
5.
   Client   *The Mary Baker Eddy Library*
              for the Betterment of Humanity
   Designer   James Silva
6.
   Client   *Indiana Interiors, LLC*
   Designer   Cynthia Schwannecke
7.
   Client   *Albuquerque Arts Alliance*
   Designers Dean Gianopoulos,
              Tom Antreasian,
              Kevin Tolman
opposite
   Design Firm **X Design Company**
   Client   *Ultimate Sailboats*
   Designers Alex Valderrama, Jen Dahlen

ULTIMATE SAILBOATS™

1.

2.

3.

4.

5.

6.

7.

8.

SOUTHERN MUSEUM OF FLIGHT

9.

DATA DIMENSIONS

10.

11.

12.

GOAHEAD

13.

Walsh & Walsh

14.

WHAT WILL YOU SAVE TODAY?

15.

1 - 8
Design Firm **Graphic Technologies**

9
Design Firm **Protective Life Creative Media**

10 - 15
Design Firm **Walsh & Associates, Inc.**

1.
Client — Medallion Group L.L.C.—Autumn Grove Condominiums
Designers — Gary Thompson, Michael Sladek

2.
Client — Harr Family Homes—Sedona
Designer — Gary Thompson

3.
Client — Lakeside Montessori
Designer — Gary Thompson

4.
Client — Medallion Group L.L.C.—Woodsong
Designer — Gary Thompson, Mary Pope-Holmes

5.
Client — Host IQ
Designers — Gary Thompson, Michael Sladek

6.
Client — One Stop Consulting Inc.
Designers — Gary Thompson, Neil Hoover

7.
Client — Issaquah Escrow
Designers — Gary Thompson, Neil Hoover

8.
Client — Snoqualmie Valley Alliance Church
Designer — Gary Thompson

9.
Client — Southern Museum of Flight
Designer — Jeff Rease

10.
Client — Data Dimensions
Designer — Miriam Lisco

11.
Client — Emotion Literacy Advocates
Designer — Miriam Lisco

12.
Client — Rotary Club of Seattle
Designer — Miriam Lisco

13.
Client — GoAhead Software
Designer — Miriam Lisco

14.
Client — Walsh & Walsh
Designers — Miriam Lisco, Teresa Walsh

15.
Client — City of Seattle—Solid Waste Utility
Designers — Miriam Lisco, Kevin Burrus

23

1.

2.

LENDING GROUP

3.

EBERHART  INTERIORS

4.

5.

6.

the
gutmann group

7.

1 - 4
Design Firm **Becker Design**
5
Design Firm **Bobby Reich-Patri GRAFIX**
6 - 7
Design Firm **Valencia Fine Design**

1.
Client   *BioForm*
Designer   Neil Becker

2.
Client   *Beta Systems*
Designer   Neil Becker

3.
Client   *GreenTree Lending Group*
Designer   Neil Becker

4.
Client   *Eberhart Interiors*
Designers   Neil Becker, Mary Eich

5.
Client   *San Francisco Beautiful*
Designer   Bobby Reich-Patri

6.
Client   *Sun Lion Press*
Designer   Mary Valencia

7.
Client   *Henning Gutmann—*
               The Gutmann Group
Designer   Mary Valencia

opposite
Design Firm **AKA Design, Inc.**
Client   *DB's Sports Bar*
Designer   Mike Mullen

DB's Sports Bar
ST. LOUIS, MO

1. **Setting the Pace**

2.

3.

4. SOUTH SHORE GRILLE
LAKE NORMAN

5. **Simply Catering**

6. **Lids for Kids**

7. RICHIE CUNNINGHAM'S **Happy Days Foundation**

8. LONE STAR BOWL

9.

™

10.

GOBBERDIEL

Jim Gobberdiel Communications

11.

Monsanto People
Leadership Team

12.

13.

generations of hope®

sm

14.

15.

1 - 8
Design Firm **Phil Evans Graphic Design Inc.**
9, 10
Design Firm **BrandLogic**
11 - 14
Design Firm **Stan Gellman Graphic Design, Inc.**
15
Design Firm **Edelman Financial Services Inc.**

1.
Client *Northeast Medical Center*
Designer Phil Evans
2.
Client *CleanAirClub.Com*
Designer Phil Evans
3.
Client *Phil Evans Graphic Design*
Designer Phil Evans
4.
Client *South Shore Grille*
Designer Phil Evans
5.
Client *Simply Catering*
Designer Phil Evans
6.
Client *WFNZ Sports Radio*
Designer Phil Evans

7.
Client *Happy Days Foundation*
Designer Phil Evans
8.
Client *Lone Star Bowl*
Designer Phil Evans
9.
Client *IBM*
Designer Alfred "Fredy" Jaggi
10.
Client *BrandLogic*
Designer Alfred "Fredy" Jaggi
11.
Client *Jim Gobberdiel Communications*
Designers Barry Tilson, Mike Donovan
12.
Client *Monsanto Company*
Designers Jill Lampen, Teresa Thompson
13.
Client *AHA!*
Designers Mike Donovan, Barry Tilson
14.
Client *Generations of Hope*
Designers Barry Tilson, Erin Goter
15.
Client *The Tavern at Great Falls*
Designer Will Casserly

1.

2.

3.

4.

Y E S H I V A   U N I V E R S I T Y   M U S E U M

5.

6.

7.

1.

2.

3.

4.

5.

6.

7.

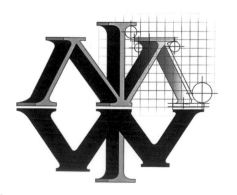

8.

9.

THE GREAT ESCAPE

10.

SOURCEONE
CREDIT UNION

11.

12.

13.

14.

15.

1, 4, 9, 12		
Design Firm	**Robert W. Taylor Design**	

2, 5
Design Firm **Heye + Partner**

3, 6, 8, 11, 14, 15
Design Firm **Englehart Dicken, Inc.**

7, 10, 13
Design Firm **1-earth Graphics**

1.
| Client | *McRel-Research into Practice* |
| Designers | Robert W. Taylor, Sandy Botello |

2.
| Client | *Ernst Kalff Obstbrennerei* |
| Designers | Norbert Herold, Martin Kiessling, Alexander Bartel, Sabine Skrobek, Wolfgang Biebach, Lothar Hackethal |

3.
| Client | *Inception* |
| Designer | Jon Cooper |

4.
| Client | *Enterprise Management Assoc.* |
| Designers | Robert W. Taylor, Yuju Liao |

5.
| Client | *Reinhold Laugallies* |
| Designers | Detlev Schmidt, Frank Widmann, Norbert Herold |

6.
| Client | *Lawrence Township Boys Basketball League* |
| Designer | Dennis Good |

7.
| Client | *Tri-County Board of Recovery & Mental Health* |
| Designer | Lisa Harris |

8.
| Client | *Indiana Machine Works* |
| Designer | Jon Lackey |

9.
| Client | *Technically Speaking, LLC.* |
| Designers | Robert W. Taylor, Rene Bobo |

10.
| Client | *Buckeye Insurance* |
| Designer | Lisa Harris |

11.
| Client | *Source One Credit Union* |
| Designer | Stephanie Freeman |

12.
| Client | *Robert W. Taylor Design* |
| Designers | Robert W. Taylor, Rene Bobo |

13.
| Client | *1-earth GRAPHICS* |
| Designers | Lisa Harris, Jay Harris |

14.
| Client | *Power 1 Credit Union* |
| Designer | Stephanie Freeman |

15.
| Client | *Mitsch Communications* |
| Designer | Paweena Lelasathaporn |

Bay Systems Integrators

1.

2.

Market!ng Concepts

3.

4.

CELEBRATION

5.

6.

NAVIGAT★R

7.

1 - 3
Design Firm **Jiva Creative**
4, 5
Design Firm **Mona MacDonald Design**
6, 7
Design Firm **Pletka Design**
1.
Client	BSI
Designer	Eric Lee
2.
Client	ArcSource
Designer	Eric Lee
3.
Client	Marketing Concepts
Designer	Eric Lee
4.
Client	eMarket Concepts
Designer	Mona MacDonald
5.
Client	Sisters of St. Joseph
Designer	Mona MacDonald

6.
Client	Nexgen Software Technologies, Inc.
Designer	Diane Pletka
7.
Client	Cova Financial Services Life Insurance
Designers	Diane Pletka, Marie Schrecengost-Carberry

opposite
Design Firm **AKA Design, Inc.**
Client	Kirkwood Parks & Recreation Department
Designer	Stacy Lanier

1.

2.

3.

4.

5.

6.

7.

8.

9.

10.

11.

12.

RIX

INDUSTRIES

13.

14.

IKOS

15.

1.

2.

Music, the language of the soul.

3.

4.

5.

6.

7.

1, 3, 5
Design Firm **Peggy Lauritsen Design Group**
2
Design Firm **LMS Design**
4
Design Firm **Shea Design**
6
Design Firm **Martin-Schaffer, Inc.**
7
Design Firm **McAdams Group**
1.
Client   *Wyoming Machine*
Designer   John Haines
2.
Client   *DeLorme*
Designer   Richard Shear
3.
Client   *Walker West Music Academy*
Designer   John Haines
4.
Client   *Shea Dairy, Inc.*
Designer   Melissa Shea

5.
Client   *Mineral Springs*
Designer   John Haines
6.
Client   *Black Rock*
Designer   Steve Cohn
7.
Client   *Mustard Seed Ranch*
Designer   Jonathan Mayer
opposite
Design Firm **The Clifford Group**
Client   *Bike Pro-Mobile*
Designer   Brian Clifford

CHIPWRIGHTS

1.

THE MALL AT

STONECREST

ATLANTA

2.

DUWAMISH
**LONGHOUSE
PROJECT**

3.

IMMUNIZE
At All Ages

4.

REDMOND ORTHODONTICS

5.

Aquatech

6.

United
EVANGELICAL FREE CHURCH

7.

TAPROOT THEATRE'S
NIGHTCAP
IMPROV
COMEDY

8.

9.

10.

Repair

11.

SENTION

12.

BlueStreak

early arrivals.com

14.

13.

STONEBRIAR
M A L L

15.

1, 11, 12, 14
Design Firm **Fassino/Design**
2, 5, 15
Design Firm **Redmond Schwartz Design**
3, 4, 7 - 9
Design Firm **Ray Braun Graphic Design**
6, 10, 13
Design Firm **DesBrow & Associates**
1.
　Client　　*Chipwrights*
　Designer　Diane Fassino
2.
　Client　　*Stonecrest Mall*
　Designer　Suzanne Schwartz
3.
　Client　　*Duwamish Tribal Services*
　Designer　Ray Braun
4.
　Client　　*Washington State Department*
　　　　　　of Health Immunization Program
　Designer　Ray Braun
5.
　Client　　*Redmond Orthodontics*
　Designer　Suzanne Schwartz
6.
　Client　　*AquaTech, Inc.*
　Designer　Brian Lee Campbell

7.
　Client　　*United*
　Designers　Jim Powell, Ray Braun
8.
　Client　　*Taproot Theatre Company*
　Designer　Ray Braun
9.
　Client　　*King's School*
　Designer　Ray Braun
10.
　Client　　*Fox Learning Systems-*
　　　　　　FarSight Brand
　Designer　Brian Lee Campbell
11.
　Client　　*Repair, Inc.*
　Designers　Diane Fassino,
　　　　　　Christianne Smith
12.
　Client　　*Sention*
　Designer　Diane Fassino
13.
　Client　　*Vocollect-BlueStreak*
　　　　　　Product Identity
　Designer　Brian Lee Campbell
14.
　Client　　*Clinician Support Technology*
　Designer　Diane Fassino
15.
　Client　　*Stonebriar Centre*
　Designer　Suzanne Schwartz

RUNet 2000

1.

2.

powerpetr●

3.

4.

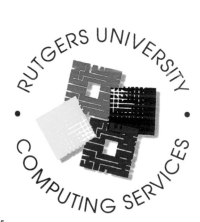

5.

6.

Newman
+ Cohen

Financial Management

7.

1, 2, 4, 5
Design Firm **Rutgers University**
3, 6, 7
Design Firm **GoldForest**
1.
Client *RUNet 2000*
Designer John Van Cleaf
2.
Client *Center for Neighborhood and Brownfields Redevelopment*
Designer John Van Cleaf
3.
Client *PowerPetro, Inc.*
Designer Sally Ann Field
4.
Client *Livingston College*
Designer John Van Cleaf
5.
Client *Rutgers Computing Services*
Designer John Van Cleaf

6.
Client *In-Formation Display Technologies, Inc.*
Designer Raymond Garcia
7.
Client *Newman and Cohen*
Designer Sally Ann Field
opposite
Design Firm **Concrete Design Communications Inc.**
Client Toronto 2008 Olympic Bid Office
Designer John Pylypczak

TORONTO

2008

1.

Circle Group
Internet Inc

2.

FOR**HEALTHY**KIDS
education encouragement guidance

3.

B&M PRINTING℠

4.

5.

S I L V E R   S A L O N

6.

BUCKLE DOWN
CLEVELAND.

Cuyahoga County Safety Belt Program

7.

Come Share the Magic

8.

42

9.

10.

11.

Rainbow
Cottages
for Kids

A SHEAR ENCOUNTER LTD
SALON & DAY SPA

12.

paint ideas.com

14.

13.

15.

PEZ LAKE DEVELOPMENT LLC

1.

2.

3.

4.

5.

SAGEWORTH

6.

7.

1, 2, 4,
Design Firm **Levine & Assoc.**

3
Design Firm **Graphica Communication Solutions**

5 - 7
Design Firm **Albert Bogner Design Communications**

1.
Client   *Pez Lake Development*
Designer   Lena Markley

2.
Client   *Tandoori Nights*
Designer   Monica Snellings

3.
Client   *Woodland Park Zoo*
Designer   Robin Walker

4.
Client   *St. Peter's Interparish School*
Designer   Monica Snellings

5.
Client   *Baltisse*
Designers   Kelly Albert, Marie Elaina Miller

6.
Client   *Sageworth*
Designer   Kelly Albert

7.
Client   *Nissley Vineyard*
Designer   Marie Elaina Miller

opposite
Design Firm **Redmond Schwartz Design**
Client   *The Promenade in Temecula*
Designers   D.J. Thomas, Suzanne Schwartz

1.

Audubon Nature Institute
Celebrating the Wonders of Nature

2.

YMCA
OF GREATER NEW YORK

150
Y E A R S
1 8 5 2 - 2 0 0 2

3.

PRECARE
for Babies
GIVING YOUR BABY THE BEST START

4.

WILLIAM & SARAH LAWRENCE SOCIETY

5.

6.

THE
LEARNING
ACADEMY

Knowledge to Succeed

7.

9

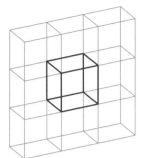

TheSquare.com

The Power of Your Network.
Squared.

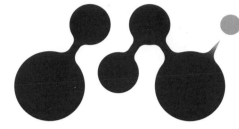

10.

9.

11.

Celebrating Rural
Georgia

12.

ITi

13.

F/ˢSTTIDE

14.

Walk A Mile
In My Shoes

15.

1, 11, 13
Design Firm **GOLD & Associates**
2, 4, 15
Design Firm **Porter Novelli**
3, 5, 6, 9, 14
Design Firm **Suka & Friends
Design, Inc.**
7, 12
Design Firm **Georgia System
Operations Corp.**
8, 10
Design Firm **Brent M. Almond**

1.
Client *South Orange Performing
Arts Center*
Designers Peter Butcavage, Joe Vavra,
Keith Gold
2.
Client *Audubon Nature Institute*
Designers Penny Rigler, Peter Buttecali
3.
Client *YMCA of Greater New York*
Designer Brian Wong
4.
Client *PreCare*
Designers Penny Rigler, Melissa Whitco
5.
Client *Sarah Lawrence College*
Designer Brian Wong

6.
Client *Barry Gordin Photography*
Designer Gwen Haberman
7.
Client *Oglethorpe Power Corporation*
Designer Brian Rickmond
8.
Client *Kelleen Griffin*
Designer Brent M. Almond
9.
Client *The Square.com*
Designer Sean Garretson
10.
Client *David Marcus*
Designer Brent M. Almond
11.
Client *Life Messages, Inc.*
Designers Keith Gold, Peter Butcavage
12.
Client *Oglethorpe Power Economic
Development*
Designer Harry Ankeny
13.
Client *I. T. I. Marketing, Inc.*
Designers Keith Gold, Peter Butcavage
14.
Client *Fasttide*
Designer Sean Garretson
15.
Client *Children's Hospital*
Designer Penny Rigler

1.

2.

3.

4.

5.

6.

7.

1, 4
Design Firm **G2 Alliance**
2, 7
Design Firm **P-2 Communications Services Computer Sciences Corporation**
3
Design Firm **Kontrapunkt**
5, 6
Design Firm **Zyrex, Inc.**
1.
Client *Donnelley Marketing*
Designer Larry Teolis
2.
Client *Computer Sciences*
Designer Bryn Farrar
3.
Client *Kontrapunkt (Slovenia)*
Designer Eduard cehovin
4.
Client *Donnelley Marketing*
Designer Larry Teolis

5.
Client *Brandable*
Designer Erika Kao
6.
Client *Metropolitan Cooporative Library System*
Designer Erika Kao
7.
Client *P-2 Communications Services Computor Sciences Corporation*
Designer Francois Fontaine
opposite
Design Firm **Concrete Design Communications Inc.**
Client *Hydro One*
Designer John Pylypczak

1.

2.

3.

4.

SHU UEMURA BOUTIQUE'S BIRTHDAY

5.

6.

7.

8.

9.

10.

ThayerDesign Inc.

11.

INTOUCH
SOLUTIONS

12.

t a t j a n a ALVEGAARD

13.

14. *Petite Loutre*

Squiggles and Giggles

Fun art for kids!

15.

1.

2.

Ruetschle Architects

3.

nurturing
nature

4.

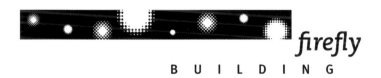

firefly
B U I L D I N G

5.

ATHLETES
in action

6.

7.

1 - 7
Design Firm **Visual Marketing
Associates, Inc.**

1.
Client   *Epic International*
Designers   Joel P. Warneke, Greg Fehrenbach

2.
Client   *Airborne Bicycles*
Designers   Greg Fehrenbach, Joel Warneke

3.
Client   *John Ruetschle Associates*
Designers   Amy Baas, Steven Goubeaux

4.
Client   *Wegerzyn Children's Garden*
Designers   Amy Baas, Kenneth Botts

5.
Client   *Cre8ive Dayton*
Designers   Kenneth Botts, Jen Dutcher,
            Al Hidalgo

6.
Client   *Athletes In Action*
Designers   Steven Goubeaux, Al Hidalgo

7.
Client   *Airborne Bicycles*
Illustrator   Joel Warneke
Typographer Greg Fehrenbach
opposite
Design Firm **Indiana Design Consortium, Inc.**
Client   *Spectrum Technologies, Inc.*
Designer   Debra Pohl Green

KEEPING YOU ORGANIZED

1.

2.

imaginative solutions.

with Kathaleen Hanna

3.

THE chamber music society of MINNESOTA

4.

THE UNIVERSITY OF TOLEDO

5.

Seattle Architectural Foundation

6.

Seattle Architectural Foundation

7.

Seattle Architectural Foundation

8.

9.

10.

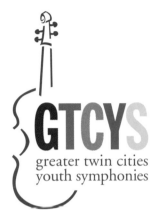

11.

12.

13.

14.

15.

1, 4, 10 - 12, 15
Design Firm **Tilka Design**
2, 6 - 9
Design Firm **Michael Courtney Design**
3, 5, 13, 14
Design Firm **Hoeck Associates, Inc.**
1.
Client   *Smead*
2.
Client   *Fleischmann Office Interiors*
Designers   Mike Courtney, Dan Hoang,
           Heidi Favour, Brian O'Neill
3.
Client   *VT Entertainment*
Designer   Marcia Hoeck
4.
Client   *The Chamber of Music Society*
Designer   Sarah Steil
5.
Client   *The University of Toledo*
Designers   Linda Szyskowski, Rosie Boger,
           Diane Ball
6, 7, 8.
Client   *Seattle Architectural Foundation*
Designers   Mike Courtney, Scott Souchock,
           Dan Hoang
Photographer
           Ted Grudowski

9.
Client   *Vulcan Northwest*
           (505 Union Station)
Designers   Mike Courtney, Scott Souchock
10.
Client   *hk portfolio*
Designer   Shannon Shriver
11.
Client   *GTCYS*
Designer   Tamatha Schneider
12.
Client   *MCCA (Mississippi Corridor*
           Community Alliance)
Designer   Micheal Wallner
13.
Client   *VT Entertainment*
Designer   Linda Szyskowski
14.
Client   *Junior League/Toledo Chapter*
Designers   Marcia Hoeck, Linda Szyskowski,
           Diane Ball
15.
Client   *Imation*

1.

2.

3.

4.

5.

6.

7.

1 - 7

Design Firm **Zunda Design Group**

1.
Client   *Tear of the Clouds, LLC*
Designers Todd Nickel, Charles Zunda

2.
Client   *B+G Foods, Inc.*
Designer Charles Zunda

3.
Client   *New England Brewing Company*
Designers Todd Nickel, Charles Zunda

4.
Client   *Newman's Own Inc.*
Designers Charles Zunda, Todd Nickel,
     Maija Riekstins

5.
Client   *Playtex Products, Inc.*
Designers Todd Nickel, Charles Zunda

6.
Client   *World Finer Foods, Inc.*
Designers Todd Nickel, Charles Zunda

7.
Client   *GAA Corporation*
Designer Todd Nickel

opposite

Design Firm **Zunda Design Group**
Client   *GAA Corporation*
Designer Todd Nickel

The ORIGINAL Shows from Radio's Most Famous Western

5 COMPACT DISCS

56 PAGE BOOK

THE LONE RANGER CHRONICLES

LIMITED COLLECTOR'S SET EDITION

A fiery horse with the speed of light, a cloud of dust and a hearty "Hi-Yo, Silver"

1.

PLISE DEVELOPMENT & CONSTRUCTION

2.

3.

4.

5.

6.

7.

8.

58

9.

10.

11.

brand.

12.

13.

redHookreads

14.

vertical
properties group

15.

1.

2.

3.

4.

5.

6.

7.

1 - 3
Design Firm **INC 3**
4 - 7
Design Firm **Wages Design**
1.
   Client   *Elara Diamonds*
   Designers Harvey Appelbaum,
             Steve Swingler
2.
   Client   *Centurion Jewelry*
   Designers Harvey Appelbaum,
             Steve Swingler
3.
   Client   *Internet Services Center*
   Designers Harvey Appelbaum,
             Christopher Nystrom
4.
   Client   *ObjectStorm*
   Designer   Diane Kim
5.
   Client   *UPC (Utilities Protection Center)*
   Designer   Matt Taylor

6.
   Client   *Arris*
   Designer   Joanna Tak
7.
   Client   *AIGA Big Night (Atlanta)*
   Designer   Dominga Lee
opposite
   Design Firm **Zunda Design Group**
   Client   *Playtex Products, Inc.*
   Designers Todd Nickel, Charles Zunda

1.

2.

3.

4.

5.

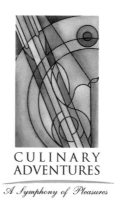

6.

7.

8.

9.

10.

11.

12.

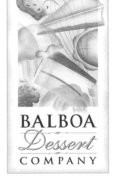

13.

14.

15.

1, 4, 6, 7, 11, 13, 14
Design Firm **On the Edge Design**
2, 3, 5, 8, 9, 12, 15
Design Firm **Wizards of the Coast**
10
Design Firm **EPOS, Inc.**

1.
Client   *Pravda*
Designers   Jeff Gasper, Gina Mims

2.
Client   *D&D Color Logo*
Designers   Dawn Murin, Matt Adelsperger,
     Sherry Floyd, Todd Lockwood
Illustrator   Henry Higgenbotham

3.
Client   *M.T.G. Player Rewards Logo*
Designers   Melissa Rapier, Mark Painter

4.
Client   *Partners Bistro*
Designers   Jeff Gasper, Tracey Lamberson

5.
Client   *M.T.G. Academy*
Designers   John Casebeer, Jeremy Bills

6.
Client   *Culinary Adventures*
Designers   Jeff Gasper, Gina Mims,
     Nicole Geiger Brown

7.
Client   *Fire & Ice*
Designers   Jeff Gasper, Gina Mims

8.
Client   *Odyssey Logo*
Designers   Corey MaCourek, Ron Spears

9.
Client   *Torment Logo*
Designers   Jen Ponce, Laurie Shattuck,
     Jason Starling

10.
Client   *Balize.com, Inc.*
Designers   Eric Martinez, Clifford Singontiko

11.
Client   *The Cabana*
Designers   Jeff Gasper, Tracey Lamberson

12.
Client   *Deckmasters Logo*
Designers   Jason Starling, Ron Spears

13.
Client   *Balboa Dessert*
Designers   Jeff Gasper, Nicole Geiger-Brown

14.
Client   *Spankies Italian Cafe*
Designers   Jeff Gasper, Tracey Lamberson

15.
Client   *Forgotten Realms Logo*
Designers   Robert Raper, Robert Campbell,
     Todd Lockwood

New Leaf
Career Solutions

1.

BioNexus Foundation

**Connecting
Global Life Science**

2.

electric stock

3.

Guitardəd

4.

5.

STEADYHOLD

the balance of science and tradition

6.

7.

1 - 3
Design Firm **Stephen Loges
Graphic Design**
4
Design Firm **VNO**
5
Design Firm **The Creative Mind**
6, 7
Design Firm **Basler Design Group**

1.
Client *New Leaf Career Solutions*
Designer Stephen Loges
2.
Client *BioNexus Foundation*
Designer Stephen Loges
3.
Client *Jim Barber Studio/
Electric Stock*
Designer Stephen Loges
4.
Client *Guitarded*
Designer Jim Vienneau

5.
Client *Team Voodoo Cycling Club*
Designer Dan Schuster
6.
Client *Steadyhold*
Designers Dan Schuster, Bill Basler
7.
Client *Phelan's Interiors*
Designers Bill Basler, Drew Davies
opposite
Design Firm **Harbauer Bruce
Nelson Design**
Client *Ace Hardware*
Designer Larry Teolis

1.

2.

3.

4.

5.

6.

7.

8.

9.

10.

11.

SEAFOOD MARKET & GRILL

12.

13.

LIDO DINER

Serving Contemporary Nostalgia

14.

CIBOLA

15.

1, 3 - 6, 9, 12, 14,
Design Firm **Unigraphics, Inc.**
2, 7, 8, 10, 11, 13, 15
Design Firm **Gardner Design**

1.
Client   *Michael Jenkins*
Designers   Jack Evans, Bonnie Evans,
            Clay McClure

2.
Client   *Plazago*
Designer   Bill Gardner

3.
Client   *K•DO*
Designers   Jack Evans, Bonnie Evans,
            Clay McClure

4.
Designers   Jack Evans, Bonnie Evans,
            Clay McClure

5.
Client   *Gerry Angeli*
Designers   Jack Evans, Bonnie Evans,
            Clay McClure

6.
Client   *Michael Ruff*
Designers   Jack Evans, Bonnie Evans,
            Clay McClure

7.
Client   *Hoch Haus*
Designer   Bill Gardner

8.
Client   *Balance*
Designer   Brian Miller

9.
Client   *Paul Morrisey*
Designers   Jack Evans, Bonnie Evans,
            Clay McClure

10.
Client   *Vizworx*
Designer   Bill Gardner

11.
Client   *Saffelli Coffee House*
Designer   Travis Brown

12.
Client   *Ed Cervantes*
Designers   Jack Evans, Bonnie Evans,
            Clay McClure

13.
Client   *Safe Temp*
Designer   Chris Parks

14.
Client   *Jim Duda*
Designers   Jack Evans, Bonnie Evans,
            Clay McClure

15.
Client   *Cibola*
Designer   Chris Parks

1.

PAINT MANAGEMENT
C O M P A N Y ,   L T D .

2.

TELE PLACE

3.

CASTILE
VENTURES

4.

5.

6.

7.

1, 2
Design Firm **Unigraphics, Inc.**
3, 4, 6
Design Firm **Gee & Chung Design**
5, 7
Design Firm **Levy Restaurants**
1.
   Client   *Nancy Marshall*
   Designers Jack Evans, Bonnie Evans,
                   Clay McClure
2.
   Client   *Richard Ainesworth*
   Designers Jack Evans, Bonnie Evans,
                   Clay McClure
3.
   Client   *TelePlace*
   Designer   Earl Gee
4.
   Client   *Castile Ventures*
   Designers Earl Gee, Fani Chung

5.
   Client   *PNC Park (PBC Grill)*
   Designer   Kirsten Mentley
6.
   Client   *Netigy Corporation*
   Designers Earl Gee, Kay Wu
7.
   Client   *Le Meridien (Cerise)*
   Designer   Kirsten Mentley
opposite
   Design Firm **Sayles Graphic Design**
   Client   *ABN AMRO "Passage to the*
                   Adventure of Life"
   Designer   John Sayles

1.

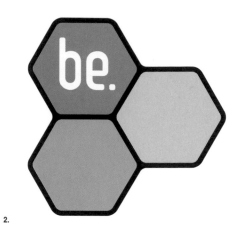

2.

3.

4.

5.

6.

7.

1, 3, 4,
Design Firm **Jasper & Bridge Assoc.**
2, 6, 7
Design Firm **be.design**
5
Design Firm **Gardner Design**

1.
Client   *Michael Charek Architects*
Designer   Kim Noyes

2.
Client   *be.design*
Designers   Eric Read, Yusuke Asaka,
            Will Burke

3.
Client   *Nors Sport*
Designer   Alexander Bridge

4.
Client   *New England American
            Institute of Architects*
Designer   Kim Noyes

5.
Client   *Crestview Plaza*
Designer   Bill Gardner

6.
Client   *Corrigo*
Designers   Eric Read, Yusuke Asaka,
            Will Burke

7.
Client   *Brian Olson Memorial
            Golf Classic*
Designers   Eric Read, Yusuke Asaka,
            Will Burke

opposite
Design Firm **Indiana Design
            Consortium, Inc.**
Client   *Spectrum Technologies, Inc.*
Designers   Debra Pohl Green, Steve Miller

Chlorophyll Meter

1.

2.

3.

FIDEL BISTRO

4.

CARLTON

P L A N T S

5.

6.

SOMNOGRAPH

7.

1, 2, 4, 6, 7
Design Firm **Gardner Design**
3
Design Firm **Dever Designs**
5
Design Firm **PA2 Design Group**

1.
Client   *Virtual Focus*
Designer   Chris Parks
2.
Client   *Richmond Raceway*
Designer   Travis Brown
3.
Client   *Development Alternatives Inc.*
Designer   Jeffrey L. Dever
4.
Client   *Fidel Bistro*
Designer   Travis Brown
5.
Client   *Carlton Plants*
Designer   Von R. Glitschka

6.
Client   *Buzz Cuts Maximum Lawncare*
Designer   Bill Gardner
7.
Client   *Somnograph*
Designers   Bill Gardner, Brian Miller
opoosite
Design Firm **be.design**
Client   *Cost Plus World Market*
Designers   Eric Read, Coralie Russo

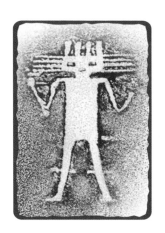

ATACAMA

1.

2.

3.

4.

5.

6.

7.

8.

PIVOTAL
TRAINING CENTER

9.

10.

S E A C L I F F

11.

ismell

12.

Mr Swap.com

13.

TEZZATA ™

14.

15.

1, 11 - 13
Design Firm **be.design**
2, 3, 6, 7, 9, 10, 14
Design Firm **Gardner Design**
4, 5, 15
Design Firm **Espy Graphics**
8
Design Firm **Paz Design Group**

1.
Client   *Microsoft*
Designers   Eric Read, Yusuke Asaka, Will Burke
2.
Client   *Bredar Waggoner Architecture*
Designer   Travis Brown
3.
Client   *Donovan Transit*
Designer   Travis Brown
4.
Client   *Upper Deck Company*
Designer   Von R. Glitschka
5.
Client   *Fire Giant*
Designer   Von R. Glitschka
6.
Client   *CRC*
Designer   Chris Parks

7.
Client   *Whoburt N. Winchester*
Designer   Chris Parks
8.
Client   *Elsinore Theatre*
Designer   Von R. Glitschka
9.
Client   *Pivotal*
Designers   Chris Parks, Travis Brown
10.
Client   *Virtual Focus*
Designer   Chris Parks
11.
Client   *Cost Plus World Market*
Designers   Eric Read, Diane Hilde, Will Burke
12.
Client   *Digiscents*
Designers   Eric Read, Yusuke Asaka, Coralie Russo, Will Burke
13.
Client   *Mr. Swap*
Designers   Eric Read, Yusuke Asaka, John Meeks
14.
Client   *Burke Corporation*
Designers   Bill Gardner, Dave LaFleur
15.
Client   *Seventh Millennium*
Designer   Von R. Glitschka

GOVERNOR NELSON A. ROCKEFELLER
EMPIRE STATE PLAZA

1.

2.

DELTAGA
CONTINENTAL CAFE

3.

RUNNING WITH SCISSORS

4.

ARES

5.

6.

Kansas Joint Replacement Institute

7.

1, 3
Design Firm **The Hillier Group**
2, 5, 7
Design Firm **Gardner Design**
4, 6
Design Firm **Richard Zeid Design**
1.
Client   *State of New York Office*
                of General Services
Designers   John Bosio, Despina Raggousis
2.
Client   *Prairie Fest*
Designers   Brian Miller, Bill Gardner
3.
Client   *Astra-Merck*
Designers   John Bosio, Susan Wisniewski
4.
Client   *Running with Scissors*
Designer   Richard Zeid

5.
Client   *ARES*
Designer   Chris Parks
6.
Client   *CEE3 Design*
Designer   Richard Zeid
7.
Client   *KJRI*
Designer   Bill Gardner
opposite
Design Firm **Arnell Group**
Client   *Rockport*
Designer   Peter Arnell

ROCKPORT

1.

2.

3.

4.

5.

6.

7.

8.

9.

10.

11.

12.

13.

SPREE '01

14.

15.

1.

2.

3.

4.

5.

6.

7.

1, 4, 7
Design Firm **Gardner Design**
2, 3
Design Firm **PK Design**
5
Design Firm **Roecker Enterprises, Inc.**
6
Design Firm **Liska & Associates, Inc.**
1.
Client   *Doskocil*
Designers Bill Gardner, Brian Miller,
           Dave LaFleur
2.
Client   *Forest Home Christian
           Conference Center*
Designer   Phyllis Kates
3.
Client   *Forest Home Christian
           Conference Center*
Designer   Phyllis Kates

4.
Client   *Excel*
Designers Bill Gardner, Brian Miller
5.
Client   *Samsung Austin*
Designer   Stephanie Phan Roecker
6.
Client   *Frank Lloyd Wright
           Preservation Trust*
Designer   Anna Moore
7.
Client   *Carlos O' Kellys*
Designer   Chris Parks
opposite
Design Firm **Cassata & Associates**
Client   *Eclectic Global Eatery*
Designer   Lesley Wexler

1.

piranha

IRONWORKERS • PRESS BRAKES • SHEARS

2.

PRAIRIE
STATE • BANK

3.

eden
Promotions
Advertising Incentives & Promotional Merchandise

4.

WICHITA
festivals inc

5.

Brooklyn's

6.

Brandology
Marketing Consulting

7.

mom 'n' me designs
Gift Baskets for all occasions

8.

9.

10.

11.

12.

13.

14.

15.

1, 2, 3, 5, 10, 12
Design Firm **Gardner Design**
4, 6, 8, 9, 13, 14
Design Firm **Gabriella Sousa Designs**
7, 15
Design Firm **Design Directions**
11
Design Firm **DeMartino Design**

1.
Client   *Burke Corporation*
Designers   Bill Gardner, Dave LaFleur

2.
Client   *Piranha*
Designer   Chris Parks

3.
Client   *Prairie State Bank*
Designer   Chris Parks

4.
Client   *Eden Promotions*
Designer   Gabriella Sousa

5.
Client   *Wichita Festivals, Inc.*
Designer   Bill Gardner

6.
Client   *Brooklyn's Restaurant*
Designer   Gabriella Sousa

7.
Client   *Brandology*
Designers   Melissa Muldoon,
            Maura Mitchell

8.
Client   *Mom 'n' me Designs*
Designer   Gabriella Sousa

9.
Client   *Computechniques*
Designer   Gabriella Sousa

10.
Client   *Burke Corporation*
Designers   Bill Gardner, Dave LaFleur

11.
Client   *Chemical Bank*
Designer   Erick DeMartino

12.
Client   *Pratt Regional Medical
            Center*
Designer   Chris Parks

13.
Client   *Calliope Sound Productions*
Designer   Gabriella Sousa

14.
Client   *Kidzexchange.com*
Designer   Gabriella Sousa

15.
Client   *Siena Analytics*
Designer   Melissa Muldoon

1.

2.

3.

4.

5.

6

7.

1, 4
Design Firm **Karacters Design Group**
2, 5, 7
Design Firm **Articulation Group**
3, 6
Design Firm **Gardner Design**
1.
Client   *McDonald's*
Designers Maria Kennedy,
                 Michelle Melenchuk
2.
Client   *Highland Feather*
Designer   Joseph Chan
3.
Client   *Big Fish*
Designer   Chris Parks
4.
Client   *Caboodles Cosmetics*
Designers Maria Kennedy,
                 Michelle Melenchuk
5.
Client   *Internac*
Designer   Joseph Chan

6.
Client   *Allen's Excavating*
Designer   Chris Parks
7.
Client   *Youth Challenge*
                 International
Designers Joseph Chan,
                 David Drummond
opposite
Design Firm **Concrete Design**
                 Communications Inc.
Client   *Umbra*
Designers Claire Dawson,
                 John Pylypczak

umbra

1.

2.

3.

4.

5.

6.

7.

8.

9.

10.

11.

12.

13.

House Calls
FINE INTERIORS

14.

SJOBERG ✛ TEBELIUS

ATTORNEYS & COUNSELORS
AT LAW

15.

1, 2, 4, 11
 Design Firm **GCG**
3, 7, 13 - 15
 Design Firm **Resco Print Graphics**
5, 6, 8 - 10, 12
 Design Firm **Art O Mat Design**
1.
| Client | *McBee Homes* |
| Designer | Brian Wilburn |
2.
| Client | *XTO Energy* |
| Designer | Brian Wilburn |
3.
| Client | *River Falls Area Chamber of Commerce* |
| Designers | Hattie Thornton, Trudy Whitemire |
4.
| Client | *Expansa* |
| Designer | Brian Wilburn |
5.
| Client | *NW Member Network* |
| Designers | Jacki McCarthy, Mark Kaufman |
6.
| Client | *Greater Seattle Chamber of Commerce* |
| Designers | Jacki McCarthy, Mark Kaufman |

7.
Client	*St. Croix Trading*
Designer	Sandy Plank
Illustrator	Mark Carey
8, 9.
Client	*Sports and Events Council of Seattle/King County*
Designers	Jacki McCarthy, Mark Kaufman
10.
Client	*The Rocket*
Designers	Jacki McCarthy, Mark Kaufman
11.
Client	*Mark Brooks Golf*
Designer	Brian Wilburn
12.
Client	*Sports and Events Council of Seattle/King County*
Designers	Jacki McCarthy, Mark Kaufman
13.
Client	*Raleigh Cycle Service*
Designer	Sandy Plank
14.
Client	*House Calls*
Designer	Barb Smothers
15.
Client	*Sjoberg & Tebelius*
Designer	Trudy Whitmire

1.

2.

SMARTEGG
LEGACY

3.

4.

6.

7.

1
Design Firm **Bryan Friel**
2, 3, 5 - 7
Design Firm **Articulation Group**
4
Design Firm **Green Springs Cafe**

1.
Client   *It's a Grind*
Designers   Bryan Friel, Marty Cox
2.
Client   *Creative Performance*
Designers   Joseph Chan, Karin Fukuzawa
3.
Client   *Smart Egg*
Designer   Joseph Chan
4.
Client   *Green Springs Cafe*
Designer   Kris Kubik
5.
Client   *Royal Bank of Canada*
Designer   Joseph Chan

6.
Client   *Community Express*
Designer   Joseph Chan
7.
Client   *Piller's*
Designer   Joseph Chan
opposite
Design Firm **Interflow
             Communications Ltd.**
Client   *Pepsi Pakistan*

mj mendes
PHOTOGRAPHER

1.

2.

3.

4.

foc
Photography

5.

6.

7.

At Home
Building
Inspection
Services

8.

Save the Children's Studio
F U N D R A I S E R

9.

10.

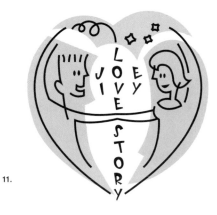

11.

caboodles®

12.

Power of 4

13.

www.barqs.com

14.

savingumoney.com™

15.

1, 2, 5, 8, 9, 13
Design Firm **Gabriella Sousa Designs**
3, 4, 6, 7, 10, 11, 14
Design Firm **Articulation Group**
12, 15
Design Firm **Karacters Design Group**

1.
Client   *MJ Mendes Photographer*
Designer   Gabriella Sousa

2.
Client   *Housefly Graphics*
Designer   Gabriella Sousa

3.
Client   *The Show Room*
Designers   Joseph Chan, Karin Fukuzawa,
              Helena Ng

4.
Client   *PearnWest*
Designer   Joseph Chan

5.
Client   *In Focus Photography*
Designer   Gabriella Sousa

6.
Client   *The Shopping Channel*
Designer   Joseph Chan

7.
Client   *Michelin*
Designers   Joseph Chan, James Ayotte

8.
Client   *At Home Building Inspection
              Services*
Designer   Gabriella Sousa

9.
Client   *Save the Children's Studio*
Designer   Gabriella Sousa

10.
Client   *Coca-Cola Ltd. (Sprite Zone)*
Designers   Joseph Chan, Craig Bond

11.
Client   *Joseph & Ivy*
Designers   Joseph Chan, Ivy Wong

12.
Client   *Caboodles Cosmetics*
Designers   Maria Kennedy, Michelle Melenchuk

13.
Client   *Power of 4*
Designer   Gabriella Sousa

14.
Client   *Coca-Cola Ltd. (Barq's)*
Designers   Joseph Chan, Karin Fukuzawa

15.
Client   *Saving U Money*
Designers   Maria Kennedy, Jeff Harrison

1.

2.

three + associates

3.

4.

ATRIUM

cafe

5.

LAND OF OZ

6.

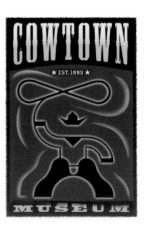

7.

1, 2, 4, 6, 7
Design Firm **Gardner Design**
3
Design Firm **Three & Associates**
5
Design Firm **Lidia Varesco Design**

1.
Client   *Chef's Pride*
Designer   Brian Miller
2.
Client   *Blue Hat Media*
Designer   Chris Parks
3.
Client   *Three & Associates*
Designers   Chris Miller, Gordon Cotton
4.
Client   *Gavin Peters Photo*
Designer   Travis Brown
5.
Client   *Levy Restaurants/*
          Indian Lakes Resort
Designer   Lidia Varesco

6.
Client   *Land of Oz*
Designer   Travis Brown
7.
Client   *Cowtown Museum*
Designer   Travis Brown
opposite
Design Firm **Sayles Graphic Design**
Client   *Christopher's*
Designer   John Sayles

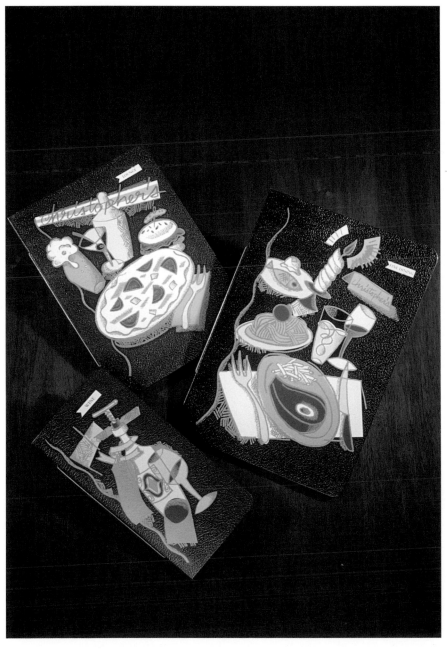

1.

2.

3.

4.

5.

6.

7.

8.

9.

10.

11.

ProperCare™

12.

CHILDREN'S ZOO

13.

UBS | PaineWebber

14.

15.

1, 2, 4, 5, 9, 12
Design Firm **In House Graphic Design, Inc.**
3, 6, 8, 11, 13, 14
Design Firm **Kiku Obata & Company**
7, 10, 15
Design Firm **Capstone Studios Inc.**

1.
Client Erie Canal Cruise Lines, Inc.
Designer Dennis J. Angelo

2.
Client Michael D. Cartner
Designer Dennis J. Angelo

3.
Client Buster Brown & Co.
Designer Scott Gericke
Illustrator Al Sacui

4.
Client Geneva Community Projects, Inc.
Designers Jeff Arbegast, Dennis J. Angelo

5.
Client Geneva Housing Authority
Designer Dennis J. Angelo

6.
Client The Mills Corporation
Designer Kathleen Roberts

7.
Client Crown Royal
Designers John Taylor Dismukes,
JoAnne Redwood

8.
Client Louisville Slugger Field
Designer Rich Nelson

9.
Client St. Peter's Episcopal
Church, Geneva, NY
Designer Dennis J. Angelo

10.
Client Coyne Beahm-Dianne Flem
Designers John Taylor Dismukes,
JoAnne Redwood

11.
Client AutoZone Park
Designer Scott Gericke

12.
Client Dr. Daniel Proper, D.D.S.
Designer Dennis J. Angelo

13.
Client St. Louis Children's Zoo
Designer Rich Nelson

14.
Client UBS Painewebber
Designers Kiku Obata, Eleanor Safe,
Paul Scherfling

15.
Client Hal Jay Green, Across Space Inc.
Designers John Taylor Dismukes,
JoAnne Redwood

1.

2.

3.

RIVER PARK SQUARE

S P O K A N E

4.

5.

B

BROWN SHOE

6.

7.

1 - 3, 7
Design Firm **Capstone Studios Inc.**
4, 6
Design Firm **Kiku Obata & Company**
5
Design Firm **Nancy Stentz Design**

1.
Client   *Ed Segura/*
              Double Eagle Casino
Designers   John Taylor Dismukes,
              JoAnne Redwood
2.
Client   *Big Inc./Steve Miles*
Designers   John Taylor Dismukes,
              JoAnne Redwood
3.
Client   *Adexd/Vista 2001*
Designers   John Taylor Dismukes,
              JoAnne Redwood

4.
Client   *River Park Square*
Designer   Scott Gericke
5.
Client   *University of California/*
              School of Arts
Designer   Nancy Stentz
6.
Client   *Brown Shoe Company*
Designers   Scott Gericke, Amy Knopf,
              Joe Floresca, Jennifer Baldwin
7.
Client   *McGraw Hill Publication*
Designers   John Taylor Dismukes,
              JoAnne Redwood,
              Jeanne Schacht

opposite
Design Firm **Sayles Graphic Design**
Client   *2000 Iowa State Fair "Zero In"*
Designer   John Sayles

1.

2.

3.

4.

5.

6.

7.

8.

9.

10.

11.

12.

13.

14.

15.

1.

2.

3.

4.

5.

6.

7.

1
Design Firm **Arcanna, Inc.**
2, 7
Design Firm **Articulation Group**
3
Design Firm **Seasonal Specialties**
4
Design Firm **Fixgo Advertising Sdn Bhd**
5
Design Firm **Indiana Design Consortium, Inc.**
6
Design Firm **Dever Designs**
1.
Client   *Bonjour: La Parisienne*
Designer   Sandra Schoultz
2.
Client   *Solect*
Designer   Joseph Chan
3.
Client   *Seasonal Specialties*
Designer   Tracy Olson

4.
Client   *EON Rally*
Designer   FGA Creative Team
5.
Client   *City of Lafayette*
Designer   Kristy Blair
6.
Client   *Brillhart Media*
Designer   Jeffrey L. Dever
7.
Client   *Coors Light*
Designer   Joseph Chan
opposite
Design Firm **Evenson Design Group**
Client   *54th Little League World
            Series 2000*
Designers   Mark Sojka, Rose Hartono
Illustrator Wayne Watford

1.

learning·com

2.

3.

FIVE STAR PROPERTIES

4.

5.

6.

7.

8.

9.

10.

11.

CANYON
HILLS

12.

13.

KEN LeGrOS
Photography

14.

P A R K L O F T

15.

1, 3 - 5, 7
Design Firm **The Wecker Group**
2, 6, 8, 9, 14
Design Firm **Dotzero Design**
10 - 13, 15
Design Firm **Sabingrafik, Inc.**

1.
Client   *John Saar Properties*
Designer   Robert Wecker
2.
Client   *Learning.com*
Designers   Karen Wippich, Jon Wippich
3.
Client   *Monterey Bay Printing*
Designers   Robert Wecker, Matt Gnibus
4.
Client   *Five Star Properties*
Designer   Robert Wecker
5.
Client   *Fasback*
Designers   Robert Wecker, Tremayne Cryer
6.
Client   *Queen of Sheba Restaurant*
Designers   Karen Wippich, Jon Wippich
7.
Client   *Bold Lions Creative
             Arts Education*
Designers   Robert Wecker, Tremayne Cryer

8.
Client   *Bonneville Environmental
             Foundation*
Designers   Jon Wippich, Karen Wippich
9.
Client   *Rulespace*
Designers   Jon Wippich, Karen Wippich
10.
Client   *South Shore*
Designer   Craig Fuller
Illustrator   Tracy Sabin
11.
Client   *Berkeley Farms*
Designer   Tim McGrath
Illustrator   Tracy Sabin
12.
Client   *Canyon Hills*
Designers   Craig Fuller, Sandra Sharp
13.
Client   *SeaCountry Homes*
Designers   Craig Fuller, Sandra Sharp
Illustrator   Tracy Sabin
14.
Client   *Ken LeGros Photography*
Designers   Jon Wippich, Karen Wippich
15.
Client   *Douglas Wilson Compainies*
Designers   Sandra Sharp, Craig Fuller
Illustrator   Tracy Sabin

1.

2.

ONE WORLD

3.

4.

5.

CarrollRacing

6.

7.

1 - 3, 6
Design Firm **The Wecker Group**
4, 5
Design Firm **Gardner Design**
7
Design Firm **Evenson Design Group**

1.
Client   *Smith Brothers*
Designers   Robert Wecker, Matt Gnibus
2.
Client   *One World*
Designer   Robert Wecker
3.
Client   *Donangelo Electric*
Designer   Robert Wecker
4.
Client   *Dewy & The Big Dogs*
Designer   Chris Parks
5.
Client   *Chuck's News Stand*
Designer   Brian Miller

6.
Client   *Carroll Racing*
Designers   Robert Wecker, Matt Gnibus
7.
Client   *Honda Corporation*
Designers   Stan Evenson, Mark Sojka
opposite
Design Firm **Power/Warner**
            Communications Group
Client   *Holtzman Corporation*
Designer   Mark Poole

1.

2.

3.

4.

5.

6.

7.

8.

9.

10.

COMPUTER DATA SOURCE

11.

12.

13.

15.

14.

1, 5, 7, 9, 10, 12, 14
Design Firm **Sabingrafik, Inc.**
2 - 4, 6,
Design Firm **The Wecker Group**
8, 11, 13, 15
Design Firm **Miravo Communications**

1.
Client — *Gator by the Bay*
Designer — Thom Podgoretsky
Illustrator — Tracy Sabin

2.
Client — *The Pebble Beach Company*
Designer — Robert Wecker

3.
Client — *Fasback*
Designers — Robert Wecker, Tremayne Cryer

4.
Client — *Gainey Suites Hotel*
Designer — Robert Wecker

5.
Client — *Sabingrafik, Inc.*
Designer — Tracy Sabin

6.
Client — *Access Monterey Peninsula*
Designer — Robert Wecker

7.
Client — *Brookfield Homes*
Designer — Craig Fuller
Illustrator — Tracy Sabin

8.
Client — *Catalyst Consulting Services*
Designer — Kanako Yamamoto

9.
Client — *Brookfield Homes*
Designer — Craig Fuller
Illustrator — Tracy Sabin

10.
Client — *Sabingrafik, Inc.*
Designer — Tracy Sabin

11.
Client — *CDS*
Designer — Steve Yasin

12.
Client — *Seafarer Baking Co.*
Designer — Tracy Sabin

13.
Client — *Kona Kofé*
Designer — Jerry Lustan

14.
Client — *Greens.com*
Designer — Dann Wilson
Illustrator — Tracy Sabin

15.
Client — *exstream*
Designer — Reece Quinones

**Textile Museum
of Canada**

1.

SECTION EIGHT

2.

HEALTH WINDS

THE HEALTH AND WELLNESS SPA

3.

azonic

NETWORKS

4.

011 LUCID 11

5.

industry.

6.

7.

atmosphere

8.

GlobalFluency

9.

Empowering Youth to End
Domestic Violence

10.

y●udai

11.

STUDIO 1/6

12.

sens com

*Your Wireless Window
To The Financial World*

13.

JOHNFRIEDMANALICEKIMMARCHITECTS

14.

CAMPION WALKER

garden design

❖

15.

1.

2.

3.

4.

5.

6.

7.

8.

9. INTERFACE

10.

11.

RENO
▶TECHNOLOGY◀

12.

13.

sm

★
VIZWORX
VISUALSOLUTIONS

14.

15.

1 - 15
Design Firm **Gardner Design**

1.
Client   *A.Little Biz*
Designer   Chris Parks

2.
Client   *Dielhman Bentwood Furniture*
Designer   Brian Miller

3.
Client   *Brain Cramps*
Designer   Brian Miller

4.
Client   *Red Devils*
Designer   Chris Parks

5.
Client   *Midwest Agricultural Board of Trade*
Designer   Travis Brown

6.
Client   *Loft 150*
Designer   Chris Parks

7.
Client   *Excel*
Designer   Chris Parks

8.
Client   *Sergeant's*
Designer   Chris Parks

9.
Client   *Interface*
Designer   Brian Miller

10.
Client   *Printmaster*
Designer   Chris Parks

11.
Client   *The Oaks*
Designer   Travis Brown

12.
Client   *Reno Technology*
Designer   Chris Parks

13.
Client   *Bavadas*
Designer   Bill Gardner

14.
Client   *Viziworx*
Designer   Chris Parks

15.
Client   *Precision Datacom*
Designer   Travis Brown

1.

2.

THINKSTREAM

3.

4.

DIGITAL  PLANET™

5.

6.

7.

9

9.

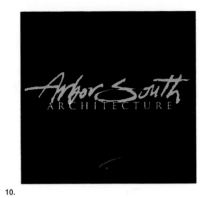

10.

Tanja Hausner

Kostümdesigns

11.

12.

e-fundresearch.com

14.

Mühlbauer

13.

FRIENDS

OF LOS GATOS PUBLIC LIBRARY

15.

1, 2, 6		
Design Firm	**Z•D Studios**	
3 - 5, 7		
Design Firm	**DotZero Design**	
8		
Design Firm	**Davies Associates**	
9		
Design Firm	**Desbrow & Associates**	
10		
Design Firm	**Funk & Associates**	
11 - 14		
Design Firm	**motterdesign, Siegmund Motter**	
15		
Design Firm	**Patt Mann Berry Design**	

1.
Client   *Green Bay Packers*
Designers   Tina Remy, Mark Schmitz

2.
Client   *Polar Sports*
Designers   Tina Remy, Mark Schmitz

3.
Client   *Thinkstream*
Designers   Jon Wippich, Karen Wippich

4.
Client   *Anita Whitesel*
Designers   Karen Wippich, Jon Wippich

5.
Client   *Digital Planet*
Designers   Jon Wippich, Karen Wippich

6.
Client   *Green Bay Packers*
Designers   Tina Remy, Mark Schmitz

7.
Client   *Photo 2000*
Designers   Karen Wippich, Jon Wippich

8.
Client   *Bedford Outpatient Surgery Center*
Designers   Cathy Davies, Drew Padrutt

9.
Client   *Vocollect—Talkman*
Designers   Susan Rupert, Brian Lee Campbell

10.
Client   *Arbor South Architecture*
Designer   Chris Berner

11.
Client   *Mrs. Tanja Hausner*
Designer   Siegmund Motter

12.
Client   *DAVID-optics*
Designer   Siegmund Motter

13.
Client   *Mühlbauer*
Designer   Siegmund Motter

14.
Client   *e-fundresearch.com*
Designer   Siegmund Motter

15.
Client   *Friends of Los Gatos Public Library*
Designer   Patt Mann-Berry

DATABASICS
Stay Ahead

1.

MIRAVO®
COMMUNICATIONS

2.

Country
Home
Mortgage

Home Finance Division of Valley Farm Credit

3.

SUPR**TEK**

4.

INTERSECT™
S O F T W A R E

5.

VALORSystems

6.

ActiveInnovations

7.

TrustCheck®

8.

114

CORBETT
T E C H N O L O G I E S

9.

**BUSINESS
APPRECIATION WEEK**
Saluting those who make Virginia work

10.

Converging Payments

11.

WAYSIDE
T H E A T R E
—Celebrating 40 years—

12.

CHINATOWN
restaurant

13.

Knowledge Based Systems

14.

15.

1, 2, 4 - 9, 11, 14
Design Firm **Miravo Communications**
3, 10, 12, 13, 15
Design Firm **Power/Warner
Communications Group**

1.
Client *Databasics*
Designer Kanako Yamamoto
2.
Client *Miravo Communications*
Designer Jerry Lustan
3.
Client *Valley Farm Credit*
Designer Mark Poole
4.
Client *Suprtek*
Designer Steve Yasin
5.
Client *Intersect Software*
Designer Kanako Yamamoto
6.
Client *Valor Systems*
Designer Kanako Yamamoto
7.
Client *info Router*
Designer Kanako Yamamoto

8.
Client *Global Integrity*
Designer Steve Yasin
9.
Client *Corbett Technologies*
Designer Kanako Yamamoto
10.
Client *Virginia Department of
Business Assistance*
Designer Sharon Snyder
11.
Client *Alogent*
Designer Jerry Lustan
12.
Client *Wayside Theatre*
Designer Mark Poole
13.
Client *Chinatown Restaurant*
Designer Josie Fertig
14.
Client *Knowledge-Based Systems*
Designer Kanako Yamamoto
15.
Client *Terra Cotta Kitchen*
Designer Mark Poole

1.

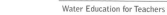

2.

3.

4.

Alcott Routon

Direct. Results.

5.

6.

7.

1 - 3, 6
Design Firm **Tribe Design, Inc.**
4, 5, 7
Design Firm **VNO**
1.
   Client   *Third Arm Solutions*
   Designers Francisco Rios, Aramis Nunez
2.
   Client   *Council for Environmental Education*
   Designers Francisco Rios, Patrick Racelis
3.
   Client   *Diagnostic Marketing Group*
   Designers Kristen Rubin, Aramis Nunez
4.
   Client   *Ryman Auditorium*
   Designer Jim Vienneau
5.
   Client   *Alcott Routon*
   Designer Jim Vienneau

6.
   Client   *Houston Used Car Network*
   Designers Francisco Rios, Aramis Nunez
7.
   Client   *Tembo*
   Designer Jim Vienneau
opposite
   Design Firm **Capstone Studios Inc.**
   Client   *Hilly Pitzer/People Magazine*
   Designers John Taylor Dismukes,
                  JoAnne Redwood

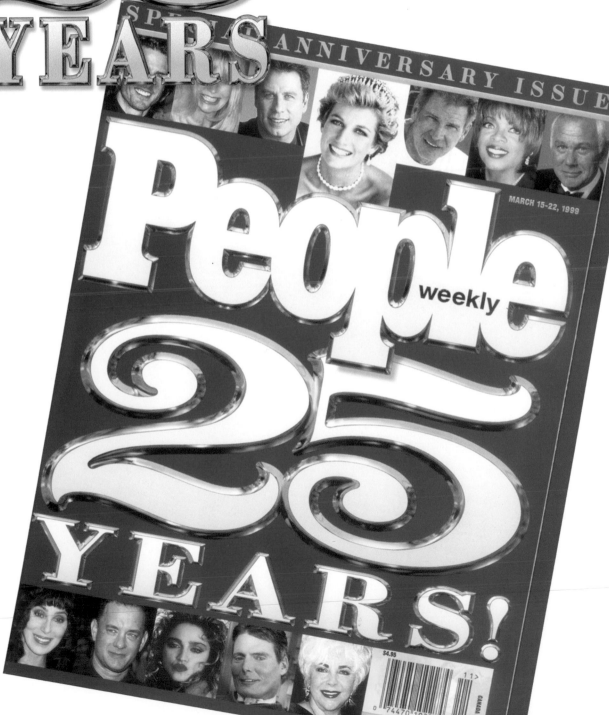

People weekly

25 YEARS

SPECIAL ANNIVERSARY ISSUE

MARCH 15-22, 1999

People weekly

25 YEARS!

$4.95

CANADA $5.95

AOL Keyword: People

0 74470 10227 4

1 1>

1.

2.

BETHEL
CONSTRUCTION

3.

4.

PiNCkNeY
P H O T O G R A P H Y

5.

6.

RIVER RANCH VINEYARDS

7.

8.

hullaballoo
bold american cooking

9.

10.

Properties, Inc.

11.

12.

13.

CENTENNIAL OF FLIGHT

1903 - 2003

14.

A Journey Through Our Solar System

15.

1 - 13		
Design Firm	**The Wecker Group**	
14, 15		
Design Firm	**Groff Creative, Inc.**	

1.		
Client	*Couture Events*	
Designer	Robert Wecker	
2.		
Client	*Traveleze.com*	
Designer	Robert Wecker	
3.		
Client	*Bethel Construction*	
Designers	Robert Wecker, Tremayne Cryer	
4.		
Client	*Carmel by the Sea.com*	
Designer	Robert Wecker	
5.		
Client	*Pinckney Photography*	
Designer	Robert Wecker	
6.		
Client	*Inns of California*	
Designer	Robert Wecker	
7.		
Client	*River Ranch Vineyards*	
Designer	Robert Wecker	

8.	
Client	*Monterey Cowboy Poetry & Music Festival*
Designer	Robert Wecker
9.	
Client	*Hullaballoo*
Designer	Robert Wecker
10.	
Client	*Wendy Dean Productions*
Designer	Robert Wecker
11.	
Client	*Di Nuovo Properties, Inc.*
Designer	Robert Wecker
12.	
Client	*City of Monterey, Ca.*
Designer	Robert Wecker
13.	
Client	*Monterey Country Inn*
Designer	Robert Wecker
14.	
Client	*Centennial of Flight Commission*
Designer	Jay Groff
15.	
Client	*Smithsonian Institution Traveling Exhibit Service, Challenger Center for Space Science Education and National Aeronautics and Space Administration*
Designer	Jay Groff

1.

2.

3.

4.

5.

6.

7.

8.

9.

10.

11.

EST. 1999

GREATLODGE

12.

élan

13.

SimplyShe

14.

newenergy

15.

1.

encore

2.

3.

4.

5.

6.

7.

8.

9.

10.

11.

12.

townhallAMERICA.com

13.

14.

15.

1 - 3, 5, 9, 10, 12 - 14
  Design Firm **MFDI**
4, 6 - 8, 11, 15
  Design Firm **Gardner Design**
1.
  Client   *Kingswood-Oxford School*
  Designers   Rich Hilliard, Mark Fertig
2, 3
  Client   *Encore*
  Designers   Mark Fertig, Jon Walker
4.
  Client   *Artistree*
  Designer   Brian Miller
5.
  Client   *Transtec*
  Designer   Mark Fertig
6.
  Client   *Power Reach*
  Designer   Brian Miller
7.
  Client   *Amber Lear*
  Designer   Brian Miller
8.
  Client   *Wichitas Promise*
  Designer   Brian Miller

9.
  Client   *The Golf Man*
  Designer   Mark Fertig
10.
  Client   *Mid-Pax*
  Designers   Sarah Marcis, Mark Fertig
11.
  Client   *CSRD*
  Designer   Bill Gardner
12.
  Client   *MFDI*
  Designers   Rich Hilliard, Mark Fertig
13.
  Client   *Graham Partners*
  Designers   Rich Hilliard, Mark Fertig
14.
  Client   *MFDI*
  Designer   Mark Fertig
15.
  Client   *Gardner Design*
  Designer   Bill Gardner

1.

PARKWAYS

FOUNDATION

PRIVATE FUNDING FOR PUBLIC GREATNESS

2.

3.

FYI

4.

CHICAGO
ILLINOIS

5.

WYOMING
BOOK™

Boise Cascade

6.

X-TEX

7.

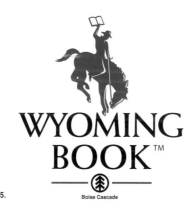

Turnberry Place

8.

Intelsat

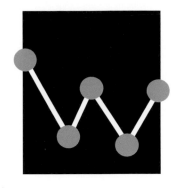

9.

Cater First

10.

E F F E R V É ®
S P A R K L I N G

11.

h 2 d

12.

TAG EX

13.

Fannie Mae
TECH PAK

14.

m i a m i
children's
m u s e u m

15.

1, 4, 5
Design Firm **Davis Harrison Dion**
2
Design Firm **Dever Designs**
3, 6
Design Firm **DGWB**
7
Design Firm **Cipriano Advertising**
8
Design Firm **Addison**
9
Design Firm **LekasMiller Design**
10, 13
Design Firm **Levine & Associates**
11, 15
Design Firm **Selbert Perkins Design**
12
Design Firm **H2D**
14
Design Firm **Graves Fowler Associates**

1.
Client   *Parkways Foundation*
Designers   Phil Schuldt, Bob Dion
2.
Client   *Climate Institute*
Designer   Jeffrey L. Dever
3.
Client   *Toshiba EID*
Designers   Jonathan Brown, Swen Igawa
4.
Client   *Chicago Convention*
        & Tourism Bureau
Designer   Bob Dion

5.
Client   *Boise Cascade*
Designers   Brent Vincent, Phil Schuldt
6.
Client   *JAX*
Designers   Jonathan Brown, Sven Igawa
7.
Client   *Turnberry Place*
Designer   Rick Cooper
8.
Client   *Intelsat*
Designers   David Kohler, Nicolas Zentner
9.
Client   *Weinsheimer Group*
Designer   Lana Ip
10.
Client   *Cater First*
Designer   Monica Snellings
11.
Client   *Eurobubblies*
Designers   Robin Perkins, Georgia Robrecht
12.
Client   *H2D*
Designers   Joseph Hausch, Allan Haas,
        Terry Lutz
13.
Designer   Lena Markley
14.
Client   *Fannie Mae*
Designer   Victoria Q. Robinson
15.
Client   *Miami Children's Museum*
Designers   C. Selbert, K. Burke, S. Bates,
        J. Kitmitto, J. Lutz

1.

2.

3.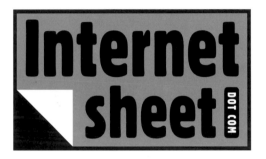

4.

5.

6.

7.

8.

9.

10.

11.

12.

13.

B O X . C O M

14.

15.

1 - 15
Design Firm **MFDI**

1.
Client Bird Play
Designers Rich Hilliard, Mark Fertig

2.
Client Comptrends, USA
Designer Mark Fertig

3.
Client Internet Sheet.com
Designer Mark Fertig

4.
Client eBone
Designer Mark Fertig

5.
Client Labels-R-Us
Designers Kevin Pitts, Mark Fertig

6.
Client Jaco Industrials
Designer Mark Fertig

7.
Client True Logic
Designer Mark Fertig

8.
Client Giftline
Designer Mark Fertig

9.
Client Paint Jockeys
Designer Mark Fertig

10.
Client MFDI
Designers Trudy Ha, Mark Fertig

11.
Client Opportunity.com
Designer Mark Fertig

12.
Client Tiger Brands
Designer Mark Fertig

13.
Client Web Traffic.com
Designer Mark Fertig

14.
Client Box.com
Designer Mark Fertig

15.
Client 4 Fun Travel Agency
Designer Mark Fertig

1.

2.

3.

handmade in italy

4.

salvage.com

5.

Developing Successful Student–Athletes & Sports Programs

6.

7.

8.

Art*iculate*
FINE ART PUBLISHING

9.

10.

Dancing With The Mouse

11.

Art*iculate*
FINE ART PUBLISHING

12.

Art*iculate*
FINE ART PUBLISHING

13.

14.

MINNESOTA
STAR OF
THE NORTH
STATE GAMES

15.

1, 3
Design Firm **Ray Braun Graphic Design**
2, 4 - 7
Design Firm **MFDI**
8
Design Firm **Addison**
9, 12, 13
Design Firm **Robert Meyers Design**
10, 11
Design Firm **Wet Paper Bag**
Visual Communication
14, 15
Design Firm **Design Center**
1.
Client   *Berean Bible Church*
Designer   Ray Braun
2.
Client   *Solid Crystal*
Designer   Mark Fertig
3.
Client   *German Retirement Home*
Designer   Ray Braun
4.
Client   *eloise rae*
Designer   Mark Fertig
5.
Client   *xSalvage.com*
Designers Kevin Pitts, Mark Fertig
6.
Client   *Athletic Education Resources*
Designer   Mark Fertig

7.
Client   *Incipience*
Designers Rich Hilliard, Mark Fertig
8.
Client   *Clark Retail Enterprises:*
Oh! Zone
Designers Kraig Kessel, Matt Versue,
Nick Bently
9.
Client   *Articulate Inc.*
Designer   Robert Meyers
10.
Client   *TCU Visual Communication*
Program
Designer   Lewis Glaser
11.
Client   *National Dance Association*
Designer   Lewis Glaser
12.
Client   *Articulate Inc.*
Designer   Robert Meyers
13.
Client   *Articulate Inc.*
Designer   Robert Meyers
14.
Client   *Taraccino Coffee*
Designers John Reger, Todd Spichke
15.
Client   *State of Minnesota*
Designers John Reger, Dan Olson

1.

2.

3.

4.

5.

6.

7.

8.

CHRISTMAS CAROL

9.

Chills and Thrills

10.

KIDS.NET

11.

Big River

THE ADVENTURES
OF HUCKLEBERRY FINN

12.

eMarineOnline.com

SUPPLY CHAIN SOLUTIONS

13.

14.

AXIS

15.

Lyf & heilsa
APÓTEK

1.

UNIVERSITY INN
AND CONFERENCE CENTER
AT RUTGERS

2.

World Tours

3.

ipro

4.

A

ACTORS THEATER
OF MINNESOTA

5.

GOTHAM

6.

OPINN SKÓGUR

7.

fried Bananas
CUBAN FOOD

8.

9.

11.

13.

15.

10.

Princeton Leadership Consulting, LLC.
Your Catalyst for Business Solutions

12.

HAGE FINANCIAL SERVICES INC.
INNOVATIVE FINANCING SOLUTIONS FOR BUSINESS.

14.

1.

2.

3.

4.

EE**Z**EE

C O M B & S T Y L E

5.

Arlington **Million**
Room

6.

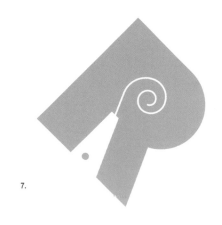

7.

8.

R2wow.com

9.

10.

OneSpiritOneWorld Inc.

*heart*strings

11.

THE
LINE DRIVE
★ Est. 2001

12.

AVIATOR'S *grill*

13.

the
Flight deck

14.

15.

1.
FRJÁLSI
FJÁRFESTINGARBANKINN

FAIRFAX
C O R N E R

2.

3.

MUSEUMS & SPECIAL EVENTS

4.

THREE RIVERS RAMBLER

5.

CHEETAH™

6.

7.

8.

9.

10.

11.

12.

14.

The Orthopædic Group
13.

15.

GPS

1.

2.

3.

4.

SunCoke
Company

5.

Ajunto®
Get iT.™

6.

SMIZER DESIGN

7.

GOODSPEED
MUSICALS

8.

9.

P R I S M
Color Corporation

10.

Confidence/Plus™

11.

Strategic
Alliances

12.

interactive d4

13.

BOX
OFFICE

14.

15.

1, 7, 8, 12, 15
  Design Firm **Smizer Design**
2 - 4, 9,
  Design Firm **Eisenberg and Associates**
5, 6, 10, 11, 13, 14
  Design Firm **D4 Creative Group**
1.
  Client   *Pfizer Inc.*
  Designer   Mark Dullea
2.
  Client   *Blockbuster Video/*
              Story Garden Productions
  Designer   Dona Mitcham
3.
  Client   *St. James Bay*
  Designer   Dona Mitcham
4.
  Client   *Moon Doggie*
  Designer   Marcus Dickerson
5.
  Client   *SunCoke Company*
  Designer   Wicky W. Lee
6.
  Client   *Ajunto*
  Designer   Wicky W. Lee

7.
  Client   *Smizer Design*
  Designers   Mark Dullea, Karl Smizer
8.
  Client   *Goodspeed Musicals*
  Designers   Karl Smizer, Steve Anderson
9.
  Client   *Atlas Scrap*
  Designer   Roger Ferris
10.
  Client   *Prism Color Corporation*
  Designer   Wicky W. Lee
11.
  Client   *Confidence Plus*
  Designer   Wicky W. Lee
12.
  Client   *Pfizer Inc.*
  Designer   Mark Dullea
13.
  Client   *iD4*
  Designer   Wicky W. Lee
14.
  Client   *Box Office*
  Designer   Wicky W. Lee
15.
  Client   *General Dynamics*
              Electric Boat
  Designer   Mark Dullea

1.

2.

WORK
REDESIGN

3.

Discovery Technology Center
Cambridge, Massachusetts

4.

Montessori
Children's House of Valley Forge

5.

EMERALD
Advisers, Inc.

6.

7.

8.

9.

10.

11.

STRATEGIC
WORKFORCE SOLUTIONS

12.

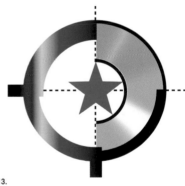

13.

MISSION: 47TH ANNUAL CONFERENCE
POSSIBLE KAB

14.

15.

1, 4, 7
Design Firm **Smizer Design**
2
Design Firm **McGraw & McGraw**
3
Design Firm **Starlight Advertising Pte Ltd**
5, 6
Design Firm **D4 Creative Group**
8
Design Firm **Interbrand Hulefeld**
9, 10, 13
Design Firm **Vasco Design**
11
Design Firm **Courtlink Creative Services**
12, 14
Design Firm **Taylor Design**
15
Design Firm **Invision Design**

1.
Client   *Armed Forces Brewmasters*
Designers   Steve Anderson, Karl Smizer
2.
Client   *Iceland Saga Travel*
Designers   Michael S. McGraw, Greg Apicella
3.
Client   *Singapore Productivity and Standards Board*
Designers   Liew Ai Lin, Wong Yin Kong
4.
Client   *Pfizer Inc.*
Designers   Mark Dullea, Karl Smizer

5.
Client   *Montessori School*
Designer   Adrienne Wright
6.
Client   *Emerald Advisers, Inc.*
Designer   Wicky W. Lee
7.
Client   *Goodspeed Musicals*
Designers   Steve Anderson, Karl Smizer
8.
Client   *Deer Run Country Club*
Designer   Christian Neidhard
9.
Client   *Museum of Contemporary Arts*
Designers   Pierre Galea, Vasco Ceccon
10.
Client   *Montreal International*
Designer   Francine Leger
11.
Client   *Courtlink Corporation*
Designer   Jonathan Georgopulos
12.
Client   *Strategic Workforce Solutions*
Designers   Hannah Fichandler, Daniel Taylor
13.
Client   *GLG Media*
Designers   Pierre Galea, Vasco Ceccon
14.
Client   *Mission Possible*
Designers   Ann Obringer, Daniel Taylor
15.
Client   *Lextel Communications Inc.*
Designer   Jonathan Georgopulos

1. **Corning** Orientation

2. mi casa

SAFARI TRAVEL
P L A N N E R S

3.

M E D I A S O L U T I O N S

4.

5.

ARTSfest

6.

7.

8.

9.

a festival of art

10.

BIJAN
INTERNATIONAL

11.

12.

13.

neon

14.

15.

The Express Lane to Bacterial Fingerprinting™

1.

2.

3.

4.

5.

6.

7.

8.

10.

dR

designRoomcreative

9.

11.

Pet Express
12.

RYAN + ASSOCIATES

13.

NEOSA
14.

USPC

15.

1.

2.

3.

4.

5.

6.

7.

8.

9.

10.

11.

12.

13.

14.

15.

1.

2.

FLYWHEELVENTURES

3.

4.

1CorkSt.

5.

6.

HOW YA BEAN

7.

8.

9.

10.

11.

12.

13.

14.

15.

1 - 15
Design Firm **MFDI**

1.
　Client　　Show Me Tickets
　Designer　Mark Fertig
2.
　Client　　Computer Environments
　Designer　Mark Fertig
3.
　Client　　Flywheel Ventures
　Designer　Mark Fertig
4.
　Client　　Planters Direct
　Designer　Mark Fertig
5.
　Client　　1 Cork St.
　Designers　Mike Barkley, Mark Fertig
6.
　Client　　Cookbook Creations
　Designers　Rich Hilliard, Mark Fertig
7.
　Client　　How Ya Bean?
　Designers　Mike Barkley, Mark Fertig

8.
　Client　　Golden Wonder
　Designer　Mark Fertig
9.
　Client　　Grassy Hill
　Designer　Mark Fertig
10.
　Client　　Debate Coach
　Designers　Kevin Pitts, Mark Fertig
11.
　Client　　Rose Murex
　Designer　Mark Fertig
12.
　Client　　Arcade Bandits
　Designer　Mark Fertig
13.
　Client　　The Eccentric Gardener
　Designer　Mark Fertig
14.
　Client　　eWorkingWomen.com
　Designers　Lindsay Ebersole, Mark Fertig
15.
　Client　　Biltmore Homes
　Designer　Mark Fertig

1.

extremetix

2.

PARK
School
TUDOR
Hall
100
YEARS OF EXCELLENCE

3.

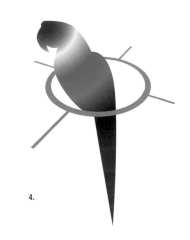

4.

AIDS Community Resources

5.

Community
&
Family
Resource Center

6.

LEADERSHIP
GREATER SYRACUSE

7.

Foxton Farm

8.

150

9.

10.

11.

12.

13.

Layer2 Networks℠

14.

HALL of FAME

Onondaga County Republican Party

15.

1, 3, 4, 6, 8 - 10, 12, 13
  Design Firm **Indiana Design Consortium, Inc.**
2, 5, 7, 11, 15
  Design Firm **adamdesign.com**
14
  Design Firm **Bright Strategic Design**

1.
  Client   *BrownDuck*
  Designer   Debra Pohl Green
2.
  Client   *extremetix.com*
  Designer   Adam Rozum
3.
  Client   *Park Tudor*
  Designers Kristy Blair, Debra Pohl Green
4.
  Client   *Parrot Press*
  Designer   Patrick Nycz
5.
  Client   *Aids Community Resources*
  Designer   Adam Rozum
6.
  Client   *Community and Family
             Resource Center*
  Designer   Kristy Blair

7.
  Client   *LGS*
  Designer   Adam Rozum
8.
  Client   *Foxton Farm*
  Designer   Amy Consdorf
9.
  Client   *Precision Putt*
  Designer   Debra Pohl Green
10.
  Client   *Lafayette Parks and Recreation*
  Designer   Debra Pohl Green
11.
  Client   *1-800-DJ*
  Designer   Adam Rozum
12.
  Client   *Slussers*
  Designer   Steve Miller
13.
  Client   *Tippecanoe Arts Federation/20th
             Anniversary of Taste of Tippecanoe*
  Designer   Kristy Blair
14.
  Client   *Layer 2 Networks*
  Designers Keith Bright, Glenn Sakamoto
15.
  Client   *Onondaga County Republican Party*
  Designer   Adam Rozum

1.

2.

3.

4.

5.

6.

7

8.

INQUISIT

9.

10.

Patera

11.

BRAZIL

on the HILL

12.

A sound design sense.

13.

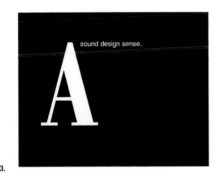

CITYNET℠

14.

FINGER LAKES WINE COUNTRY

VISITOR
C E N T E R

1.

2.

3.

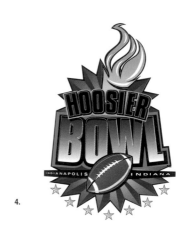

4.

Property Consultants • Property, Plant & Machinery Valuers • Real Estate Agents • Property Managers

5.

6.

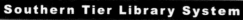

7.

8.

9.

10.

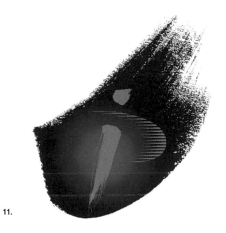

11.

12.

13.

14.

15.

1, 6, 7, 15
Design Firm **Michael Orr + Associates, Inc.**
2, 3, 5, 8, 11, 13, 14
Design Firm **Starlight Advertising Pte Ltd**
4, 9, 10, 12
Design Firm **Planet 10**

1.
Client *Finger Lakes Wine Country Visitor Center*
Designers Michael R. Orr, Thomas Freeland

2.
Client *National University of Singapore*
Designers Liew Ai Lin, Wong Yin Kong

3.
Client *Innolab Pte Ltd*
Designer Chong Yat Weng

4.
Client *Hoosier Bowl*
Designer Mike Tuttle

5.
Client *Robert Khan & Co.*
Designer Chong Yat Weng

6.
Client *Corning Museum of Glass*
Designers Michael R. Orr, Thomas Freeland

7.
Client *Southern Tier Library System*
Designer Michael R. Orr

8.
Client *Singapore Police Force*
Designer Liew Ai Lin

9.
Client *Playing Mantis*
Designers Mike Tuttle, Tina Smith

10.
Client *Jaycee's*
Designer Mike Tuttle

11.
Client *Singapore Productivity and Standards Board*
Designers Liew Ai Lin, Wong Yin Kong

12.
Client *Indiana State Museum*
Designer Jennifer Tuttle

13, 14.
Client *Singapore Productivity and Standards Board*
Designers Liew Ai Lin, Wong Yin Kong

15.
Client *Southern Tier Library System*
Designers Michael R. Orr, Thomas Freeland

1.

2.

COALITION FOR
Women's Basketball

3.

4.

GOOD
SAMARITAN
CENTER
of the Episcopal Diocese of West Texas

5.

SAN ANTONIO
SPORTS FOUNDATION

6.

7.

8.

9.

10.

11.

12.

ARTEXT ARTEXT

S_ART

14.

ARTEXT ARTEXT

13.

POPE JOHN PAUL II
• CULTURAL CENTER •

15.

1, 4
Design Firm **Set?Communicate!**
2, 5, 6
Design Firm **Creative Link**
3
Design Firm **Fraulein Design**
7
Design Firm **Di Zinno Thompson**
8
Design Firm **Wilmer Fong + Associates**
9, 12
Design Firm **Cahan and Associates**
10, 11, 13
Design Firm **Iridium, a design agency**
14
Design Firm **Michael Niblett Design**
15
Design Firm **Grafik Marketing Communications, Ltd.**
1.
Client *Mississippi Valley State University*
Designers Steve Thomas, Eric Grab
2.
Client *Coalition for Women's Basketball*
Designer Kyle Derr
3.
Client *Fraulein Design*
Designer Stacy Messerschmidt
Illustrator Tracy Sabin
4.
Client *Mississippi Valley State University*
Designers Steve Thomas, Eric Grab

5.
Client *Good Samaratin Center*
Designer Ben Reynolds
6.
Client *San Antonio Sports Foundation*
Designer Mark Broderick
7.
Client *Golden Eagle Insurance*
Designers Annie Pearson, Robin Vallaire
Illustrator Tracy Sabin
8.
Client *L'Amyx*
Designers Steve Jeong, Nina Edwards
9.
Client *NetObjects.com*
Designers Craig Bailey, Bill Cahan
10.
Client *Cambell Group*
Designers Jean-Luc Denat, Nadia Fauteux
11.
Client *ACO (Aids Committee of Ottawa)*
Designer Jean-Luc Denat
12.
Client *NetObjects.com*
Designers Craig Bailey, Bill Cahan
13.
Client *Artext*
Designers Jean-Luc Denat, Mario L'Écuyer
14.
Client *J.M. Moudy Exhibition Hall*
Designer Michael Niblett
15.
Client *Pope John Paul II Cultural Center*
Designer Michelle Mar

1.

2.

3.

4.

5.

6.

7.

8.

9.

10.

11.

12.

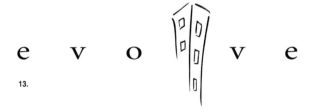

13.

14.

15.

1, 7, 8, 10 - 12, 14, 15
Design Firm **MFDI**
2 - 5, 9, 13
Design Firm **Pensaré Design Group**
6
Design Firm **CWA, Inc.**

1.
Client *Bestway*
Designer Mark Fertig

2.
Client *Jo Printz (Cuppa' Jo)*
Designer Kundia D. Wood

3.
Client *John Mangan (Mangan Group Architects)*
Designer Kundia D. Wood

4.
Client *Aventis*
Designer Kundia D. Wood

5.
Client *Jeff Printz & Chris Swanson (Otto's Suds & Duds)*
Designer Kundia D. Wood

6.
Client *Watkins Manufacturing*
Designer Scott Wyss

7.
Client *Veribuy*
Designer Mark Fertig

8.
Client *Waste Savers*
Designers Rich Hilliard, Mark Fertig

9.
Client *Richard Pellicci*
Designer Yi Hong Hsu

10.
Client *Communitools*
Designer Mark Fertig

11.
Client *Lake Michigan Water*
Designer Mark Fertig

12.
Client *Mom2B Maternity*
Designers Mike Barkley, Mark Fertig

13.
Client *Evolve Developments, LLC*
Designer Kundia D. Wood

14.
Client *Net Nooz*
Designer Mark Fertig

15.
Client *JAS*
Designer Mark Fertig

1.

2.

LASERPACIFIC

MEDIA CORPORATION

3.

KINZAN

4.

5.

WATERBURY Garden

6.

VON GAL ASSOCIATES

7.

8.

KENNYBROWN

The Fusion of Performance, Engineering and Style

9.

10.

N E T I S U N ™

11.

stēl **OBJEKT**

F u r n i t u r e   f o r   t h e   S o u l

12.

4 SEASONS

· C A R   W A S H ·

13.

Volunteers

I N   M E D I C I N E

14.

OPTIONS
BY DESIGN

INCORPORATED

15.

1.

2.

3.

4.

5.

6.

7.

8.

9.

10.

11.

12.

13.

14.

15.

1 - 4, 6, 9 - 13
Design Firm **Visual Asylum**

5, 14
Design Firm **Sabingrafik, Inc.**

7, 8, 15
Design Firm **Planet 10**

1.
Client   *The Reserve*
Designer   Joel Sotelo

2.
Client   *The Reserve*
Designer   Joel Sotelo

3.
Client   *Congo Jacks*
Designer   Amy Jo Levine

4.
Client   *The Reserve*
Designer   Joel Sotelo

5.
Client   *AIRS*
Designers   James Schenck,
      David Forman
Illustrator   Tracy Sabin

6.
Client   *2 to Tango*
Designer   Joel Sotelo

7.
Client   *Radius*
Designer   Mike Tuttle

8.
Client   *Escient Convergence*
Designer   Mike Tuttle

9 - 11.
Client   *The Reserve*
Designer   Joel Sotelo

12.
Client   *Lido Peninsula*
Designer   Amy Jo Levine

13.
Client   *La Papaya*
Designer   Joel Sotelo

14.
Client   *Tamansari Beverage*
Designers   Karim Amirgani, Tracy Sabin

15.
Client   *INITA*
Designers   Jennifer Tuttle, Tina Smith

1.

2.

3.

4.

5.

6.

7.

8.

9.

10.

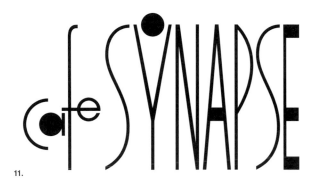

11.

12.

13.

14.

15.

1, 2, 5, 7, 8
Design Firm **Sayles Graphic Design**
3
Design Firm **Formula Creative**
4
Design Firm **FL:AT:09**
6
Design Firm **MTZ**
9, 13
Design Firm **Tangram Strategic Design**
10
Design Firm **Lieber Brewster Design**
11
Design Firm **Studio Francesca Garcia-Marques**
12, 14, 15
Design Firm **Erbe Design**

1.
Client   *McArthur Company (Enviropure)*
Designer John Sayles
2.
Client   *Sayles Graphic Design*
          (Smarty Pants)
Designer John Sayles
3.
Client   *Formula Creative*
Designer Marty Csercsevits
4.
Client   *rddm Sound Design*
Designer Johnny Gallardo
5.
Client   *Advertising Professionals*
          of Des Moines
Designer John Sayles

6.
Client   *SuzyPress Agency,*
          (Stockholm, Sweden)
Designer Mikael T. Zielinski
7.
Client   *McArthur Company (Happy Grass)*
Designer John Sayles
8.
Client   *Zook's Harley Davidson*
Designer John Sayles
9.
Client   *IFM Infomaster*
Designer Enrico Sempi
10.
Client   *New York Academy of Medicine*
11.
Client   *Café Synapse/*
          Associated Students UCLA
Designer Francesca Garcia-Marques
12.
Client   *Media Life*
Designers Maureen Erbe, Karen Nakatani
13.
Client   *Borsani Comunicazione*
Designer Enrico Sempi
14.
Client   *Landscape Development*
Designers Maureen Erbe, Rita Sowins,
          Efi Latief
15.
Client   *Southern California Edison*
Designers Maureen Erbe, Tracy Lewis

1.

SPIDER SECURITIES

2.

3.

4.

5.

6.

7.

PARC METROPOLITAN

8.

9.

10.

11.

12.

13.

visual  asylum

14.

15.

1.

2.

3.

4.

5.

6.

7.

8.

9.

10.

11.

12.

13.

College of St. Joseph

14.

15.

1 - 3, 5 - 9, 11, 13, 15
Design Firm **Mike Quon/Designation**
4
Design Firm **RTKL Associates Inc./ID8**
10, 12, 14
Design Firm **Set?Communicate!**

1.
Client | *phone vision*
Designer | Mike Quon

2.
Client | *Wired Environments*
Designers | Mike Quon, Anna Moreira

3.
Client | *AT+T*
Designers | Mike Quon, Anna Moreira

4.
Client | *Old Mutual Properties*
Designers | Greg Rose, Young Choe, Thom McKay

5.
Client | *Woody Allen*
Designers | Mike Quon, Anna Moreira

6.
Client | *Eastern Environmental*
Designer | Mike Quon

7.
Client | *Reuters*
Designer | Mike Quon

8.
Client | *Unilogic*
Designers | Mike Quon, Anna Moreira

9.
Client | *New York Life*
Designer | Mike Quon

10.
Client | *Church of the Beloved*
Designers | Steve Thomas, Dan Wold

11.
Client | *Unity Technology*
Designers | Mike Quon, Anna Moreira

12.
Client | *Omega Global*
Designers | Steve Thomas, Dan Wold

13.
Client | *The National Conference*
Designer | Mike Quon

14.
Client | *College of St. Joseph*
Designers | Steve Thomas, Dan Wold

15.
Client | *KPMG Consulting*
Designers | Mike Quon, Anna Moreira

1.

2.

3.

bellink health

4.

5.

EPPSTEIN UHEN
A R C H I T E C T S

6.

7.

QUAIL·HILL

8.

Authentic. Diverse. CALIFORNIA.

9.

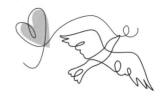

AGE CONCERNS

10.

BIO DIVERSITY

11.

12.

13.

LMP|NYC

14.

15.

1 - 5, 11, 13
Design Firm **Thiel Design**
6, 7, 14
Design Firm **LMP/NYC**
8 - 10, 15
Design Firm **Miriello Grafico**
12
Design Firm **Design North**

1.
Client — University of Wisconsin—Milwaukee athletic department
Designer — Gary Haas
Illustrator — Mike Kasun

2.
Client — Woodland Prime
Designer — Gary Haas

3.
Client — University of Wisconsin-Milwaukee
Designer — John Thiel

4.
Client — Bellin Health
Designer — John Thiel

5.
Client — Eppstein Uhen
Designer — John Thiel

6.
Client — Fresh Produce
Designer — Nina Schuermaier

7.
Client — Allied Partners Inc.
Designer — Nina Schuermaier

8.
Client — Quail Hill
Designers — Dennis Garcia, Chris Keeney

9.
Client — San Diego Conventioner's Bureau
Designer — Dennis Garcia

10.
Client — Age Concerns
Designer — Dennis Garcia

11.
Client — Biodiversity
Designer — John Thiel

12.
Client — Ertl Collectibles

13.
Client — Snap-on Inc.
Designer — John Thiel

14.
Client — LMP/NYC
Designer — Nina Schuermaier

15.
Client — Harcourt
Designer — Dennis Garcia

1. sunflower | BROADBAND

2. MAGPIE COMMUNICATIONS

3. 8CR8ATIONS

COLLEGE PLACE NUTRITION
Smoothie Supreme

4.

5. POWERTRUNK

DUPONT DENTAL
at Barksdale Station

6.

7. LOAN**TEK**
WISHES WELCOME. DREAMS APPROVED.

8. NYGEM

Sunshine Metals

9.

10.

11.

LES ALIMENTS FINS
LE DUC

12.

PlyTac

PLYWOOD TACOMA, INC.

13.

ÉCRITS DES HAUTES~TERRES

14.

15.

1.

MIKIMOTO

2.

Dch*

*theDocumentarychannel

3.

Baas & Associates PC
growing your business

4.

Willard
ON THE TOWN
catering

5.

 genesis

6.

grille

7.

cultura~

8.

9.

10.

11.

12.

13.

15.

Intercontinental Exchange

14.

1, 4
Design Firm **Dotzler Creative Arts**
2, 3, 8, 15
Design Firm **Arnell Group**
5, 7, 9, 12, 13,
Design Firm **The Campbell Group**
6, 10, 11, 14
Design Firm **Melia Design Group**

1.
Client — Trinity Interdenominational Church
2.
Client — Mikimoto
Designer — Peter Arnell
3.
Client — The Documentary Channel
Designers — Peter Arnell, Mike Doyle
4.
Client — Baas & Associates
5.
Client — The Willard Inter-Continental Hotel
Designer — Joanne Westerman
6.
Client — Genesis
Designer — Frank Chen

7.
Client — The Baltimore Marriott Waterfront Hotel
Designer — Joanne Westerman
8.
Client — Cultura
Designer — Peter Arnell
9.
Client — The Puerto Rico Convention Center
Designer — Joanne Westerman
10.
Client — Return.com
Designer — Frank Chen
11.
Client — EZ Fizz (Coca-Cola)
Designers — Shai Harris, Frank Chen
12.
Client — The Baltimore Marriott Waterfront Hotel
Designer — Joanne Westerman
13.
Client — The Willard Inter-Continental Hotel
Designer — Joanne Westerman
14.
Client — Intercontinental Exchange
Designer — Jeff Brostoff
15.
Client — Pass Entertainment
Designers — Peter Arnell, Mike Doyle

H.O.P.E.

Highmark Osteoporosis Prevention and Education Program

1.

LIDIA VARESCO

2. DESIGN

Pinnacle

AT BRICKYARD LANDING

3.

4.

RIVERMARK

of Santa Clara

5.

HIGHGROVE
AT DUBLIN RANCH

6.

7.

OUTLOOK HEIGHTS

8.

9.

11.

13.

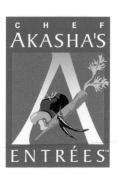

15.

Ozark Homes and Property.com

10.

Ozark Health.com

12.

Ozark Doctors.com

14.

1.

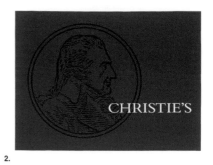

2.

3.

4.

5.

6.

7.

8.

Se·man·tix

9.

10.

HONDA RACING

11.

THE GIVING TREE

12.

13.

14. EN**S**PHERICS

IDYLLWILD JAZZ 2001 IN THE PINES

15.

1, 8, 10
Design Firm **Pandora and Company**
2
Design Firm **Carbone Smolan Agency**
3 - 5, 7, 9, 11, 12, 14, 15
Design Firm **Evenson Design Group**
6
Design Firm **Dart Design**
13
Design Firm **Janice Barrett Design**

1.
Client   *San Luis Obispo County Parks Dept.*
Designers   Stephanie Fernandez, Pandora Nash-Karner

2.
Client   *Christie's*
Designers   Claire Taylor, Sharon Slaughter Koi Vantanapahu

3.
Client   *Acura Music Festival*
Designers   Stan Evenson, Glenn Sakamoto, Jill Maida

4.
Client   *Angel City Fitness*
Designers   Stan Evenson, Mark Sojka

5.
Client   *St. Vincent Medical Center*
Designers   Stan Evenson, Judy K. Lee, John Krause

6.
Client   *Great River Golf Club*
Designers   David Anderson, Linda Anderson

7.
Client   *Honda Corporation*
Designers   Stan Evenson, Mark Sojka, John Krause

8.
Client   *San Luis Obispo County Visitor's Bureau*
Designers   Stephanie Fernandez, Pandora Nash-Karner

9.
Client   *Semantix*
Designer   Mark Sojka

10.
Client   *Los Osos Community Services District*
Designers   Cynthia Milhem, Paula Cavallara Pandora Nash-Karner

11.
Client   *Honda Corporation*
Designers   Stan Evenson, Mark Sojka, John Krause

12.
Client   *The Giving Tree*
Designers   Stan Evenson, Mark Sojka

13.
Client   *Valley Lahuosh Baking Co.*
Designer   Janice Barrett

14.
Client   *Enspherics*
Designers   Stan Evenson, Judy K. Lee Tricia Rauen

15.
Client   *Idyllwild Jazz Music Festival*
Designers   Stan Evenson, Ondine Jarl

179

1. The Evergreen Society

2. DANCE CLEVELAND

PARKWORKS

4.

white sand villas

5.

LAND ONE

6.

7.

SCHEFFLERA SUMO

8.

9.

CORPORATE SYSTEMS

10.

11.

12.

WebSiteDesigns.com

13.

BREWER&TOMINAGA

14.

15.

1.

2.

3.

4.

5.

6.

7.

8.

9.

10.

11.

12.

13.

14.

15.

2.

1.

3.

4.

5.

FANTASY

6.

M E N ' S **POOL**

The Cooper Union Annual Phonathon

2001

7.

8.

TeaM
ActiVe DreaMers™

9.

10.

11.

12.

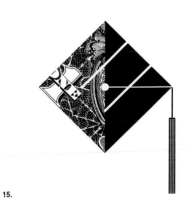

13.

14.

15.

1.

2.

3.

4.

5.

6.

7.

8.

FORTERA
Technology Assurance

9.

10.

Ovation™

11.

Alkermes
Science that Delivers

12.

R|A|M

13.

pocketDBA™

14.

west

15.

1.

2.

3.

4.

5.

6.

7.

8.

9.

EmoryVision

10.

ÖSEL

11.

DELPHI
PRODUCTIONS

12.

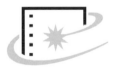

SharpShooter Spectrum
Imaging

13.

PRIMEresponse

Relationship marketing just got better.™

14.

15.

1, 3
Design Firm **Tim Kenney Design Partners**
2, 4, 6 - 9
Design Firm **Greteman Group**
5
Design Firm **LPG Design**
10
Design Firm **ThinkHouse Creative, Inc.**
11 - 15
Design Firm **Focus Design**

1.
Client — *Holy Trinity Catholic Church*
Designers — Tim Kenney, Charlene Gamba

2.
Client — *Flexjet*
Designer — James Strange

3.
Client — *Personal Communications Industry Association*
Designers — Tim Kenney, Monica Banko, Charlene Gamba

4.
Client — *Climate Works*
Designer — James Strange

5.
Client — *Gourmet's Choice Roasterie*
Designers — Lorna West, Chris West

6.
Client — *Executive Aircraft*
Designer — James Strange

7.
Client — *Flexjet*
Designer — James Strange

8.
Client — *R. Messner Construction Company*
Designer — James Strange

9.
Client — *City of Wichita*
Designer — James Strange

10.
Client — *Emory Vision*
Designer — Gregg Snyder

11.
Client — *Osel Incorporated*
Designer — Brian Jacobson

12.
Client — *Delphi Productions*
Designer — Brian Jacobson

13.
Client — *Sharpshoot Spectrum*
Designer — Brian Jacobson

14.
Client — *Prime Response*
Designer — Brian Jacobson

15.
Client — *Appearance Salon*
Designer — Brian Jacobson

189

1.

2.

3.

4.

6.

5.

7.

8.

9.

10.

11.

12.

13.

14.

MediaStorytellers

15.

1
  Design Firm **Paris Design Studio**
2, 5, 8, 11 - 14
  Design Firm **Guarino Graphics**
3, 4, 6, 7, 15
  Design Firm **Focus Design**
9
  Design Firm **Nine Design**
10
  Design Firm **Simple Green**

1.
  Client   *Joseph Vatekov Studio*
  Designer   Theresa Paris
2.
  Client   *W.D. Burson + Associates.*
  Designer   Jan Guarino
3.
  Client   *Annuncio Software*
  Designer   Brian Jacobson
4.
  Client   *ShopEaze Systems*
  Designers Brian Jacobson, Anthony Luk
5.
  Client   *Leverage Studio*
  Designer   Jan Guarino
6.
  Client   *Support Minds*
  Designers Brian Jacobson, Anthony Luk

7.
  Client   *Spectrum Photographic*
  Designer   Brian Jacobson
8.
  Client   *ecotech*
  Designer   Jan Guarino
9.
  Client   *Puget Sound Blood Center*
  Designer   Lana R. Abrams
10.
  Client   *Light + Salt Presbyterian Church*
  Designer   Wesley J. Su
11.
  Client   *DLC Leasing*
  Designer   Jan Guarino
12.
  Client   *Holliswood Care Center*
  Designer   Jan Guarino
13.
  Client   *Webline Designs*
  Designer   Jan Guarino
14.
  Client   *Continuity Centers*
  Designer   Jan Guarino
15.
  Client   *MediaStorytellers*
  Designer   Brian Jacobson

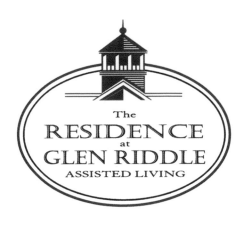

1.

2.

3.

4.

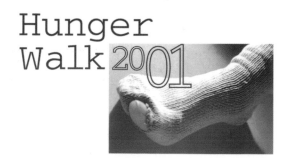

5.

6.

7.

8.

9.

10.

11.

12.

13.

14.

Les Piafs

15.

1 - 5
Design Firm **Guarino Graphics**

6
Design Firm **Fusion Art Institute**

7, 8
Design Firm **Davison Dietsch McCarthy**

9 - 14
Design Firm **Laura Coe Design Assoc.**

15
Design Firm **Belyea**

1.
Client — *The Residence at Glen Riddle*
Designer — Jan Guarino

2.
Client — *Painted Pieces Studios*
Designer — Jan Guarino

3.
Client — *Lorich Building Corp.*
Designer — Jan Guarino

4.
Client — *Z Counsel LLC.*
Designer — Jan Guarino

5.
Client — *Bentley Properties*
Designers — Jan Guarino, Tara Gordon

6.
Client — *Youga*
Designers — Fumihiko Enokido, Hideaki Enokido

7.
Client — *Grand Rapids Area
Center for Ecumenism*
Designer — Rachel Reenders

8.
Client — *Grace College*
Designers — Rachel Reenders, Kurt Dietsch

9.
Client — *Active Motif*
Designer — Thomas Richman

10.
Client — *Printing Industries Assoc.*
Designers — Laura Coe Wright, Thomas Richman

11.
Client — *Ballena Vista Farm*
Designers — Laura Coe Wright, Thomas Richman
Tracy Castle

12.
Client — *ReturnView, Inc.*
Designer — Tracy Castle

13.
Client — *JNR, Inc.*
Designer — Ryoichi Yotsumoto

14.
Client — *Active Motif*
Designer — Thomas Richman

15.
Client — *Les Piafs*
Designers — Christian Salas, Kelli Lewis

1.

2.

Northern Soles, Inc.
Casual Shoes & Boots

3.

4.

*Bird*Sight

5.

6.

SIMON **LIVE MEDIA**
N E T W O R K ™

7.

THE
Manhattan
SOCIETY

8.

Bove
COMPANY

9.

10.

11.

12.

13.

maximumscience

If you're serious about science

14.

15.

1.

2.

3.

4.

5.

6.

7.

8.

9.

10.

11.

12.

13.

14.

15.

1, 10, 12, 14
  Design Firm **30sixty design, inc.**
2, 5, 8, 13, 15
  Design Firm **Herip Associates**
3, 6, 9, 11,
  Design Firm **EHR Design**
4
  Design Firm **Tribe Design, Inc.**
7
  Design Firm **David Brodsky Graphic Design**

1.
  Client   NARAS
  Designer   Ethan Archer
2.
  Client   Cleveland Indians
  Designers   Walter M. Herip, John R. Menter
3.
  Client   Impressions
  Designer   Brian Eickhoff
4.
  Client   New Attitude Ministries
  Designers   Francisco Rios, Ruth Ann McLean
5.
  Client   Cleveland Indians
  Designers   Walter M. Herip, John R. Menter
6.
  Client   Leadership Solutions
  Designer   Carlos Zapata

7.
  Client   Templegate Publishers
  Designer   David Brodsky
8.
  Client   Cleveland Indians
  Designers   Walter M. Herip, John R. Menter
9.
  Client   The Palmer Course
  Designers   Mark Rue, Ben Reynolds
10.
  Client   Mattel
  Designers   Tom Gundred, Craig Peterson
11.
  Client   Total E Entertainment
  Designers   Brian Eickoff, Carlos Zapata
12.
  Client   Mattel
  Designer   Tom Gundred
13.
  Client   Cleveland Indians
  Designers   Walter M. Herip, John R. Menter
14.
  Client   Mattel
  Designer   Craig Peterson
15.
  Client   Cleveland Indians
  Designers   Walter M. Herip, John R. Menter

RECORDING
ACADEMY
MEMBERSHIP
AWARDS

1.

BODIES *in* BALANCE

2.

HUMANITY
through
TECHNOLOGY

3.

inVISION

4.

BINGHAM DANA

5.

CAPTIVATE™

6.

MICHIGAN

7.

BAC

BOSTON ARCHITECTURAL CENTER

8.

ROCKTAILS

9.

THE ARBORS
OF THOUSAND OAKS

10.

11.

CITIZEN SCHOOLS

12.

A?T

13.

30 adelaide e.

14.

CIRCUS BOYS

15.

1 - 4, 9, 11
Design Firm **Top Design Studio**
5 - 8, 10, 12
Design Firm **Selbert Perkins Design**
13
Design Firm **Robert Meyers Design**
14
Design Firm **Hambly + Woolley Inc.**
15
Design Firm **Michael Niblett Design**

1.
Client *The Recording Academy*
Designer Peleg Top

2.
Client *Anneliza Arnold/Bodies in Balance*
Designers Rebekah Beaton, Peleg Top

3.
Client *The Shoah Foundation*
Designer Peleg Top

4.
Client *Rashelle Westcot/InVision*
Designers Peleg Top, Rebekah Beaton

5.
Client *Bingham Dana*
Designer Josh Roy

6.
Client *Captivate Networks*
Designer Gary Pikovsky

7.
Client *Automobile National Heritage Area*
Designers Aaron Haesaert, Josh Roy,
Arvi Raquel-Santos

8.
Client *Boston Architectural Center*
Designers Sheri Bates, Jonathan Theiss

9.
Client *Doug Richter & Lisa Hopkins*
Designer Peleg Top

10.
Client *Hileman Company*
Designer Liz Choi

11.
Client *Amy Goldsmith/GK Communications*
Designers Rebekah Beaton, Peleg Top

12.
Client *Citizen's School*
Designers Sheri Bates, Gary Pikovsky

13.
Client *Is It Art?*
Designer Robert Meyers

14.
Client *Dundee Realty*
Designers Katina Constantinou,
Jayson Zaleski, Bob Hambly

15.
Client *Circus Boys*
Designer Michael Niblett

7.

3.

4.

1.

H·I·S Investmentconsulting Service GmbH

2.

5.

6.

8.

200

ADLER

9.

10.

GÖNNER+GAISSMEYER
PRÄZISIONSDREHTEILE

11.

HONBERG
SOMMER
2001

12.

13.

STADT
GEISINGEN
AN DER JUNGEN DONAU

14.

15.

1, 13
Design Firm **The Wecker Group**
2 - 7, 9, 11, 12, 14
Design Firm **revoLUZion-Studio für Design**
8, 10, 15
Design Firm **Boelts Bros. Associates**

1.
Client   *Highlands Inn Park Hyatt*
Designer   Robert Wecker

2.
Client   *HIS*
Designer   Bernd Luz

3.
Client   *Ba-Wü InLine-Cup*
Designer   Bernd Luz

4.
Client   *Paul Peschke*
Designer   Bernd Luz

5.
Client   *Cargo Team*
Designer   Bernd Luz

6.
Client   *take-off GewerbePark*
Designer   Bernd Luz

7.
Client   *Stadt Neßkirch*
Designer   Bernd Luz

8.
Client   *Nimbus Brewery*
Designers   Jackson Boelts, Brett Weber

9.
Client   *Adler*
Designer   Bernd Luz

10.
Client   *Jackson Boelts*
Designer   Jackson Boelts

11.
Client   *Gönner+Gaissmeyer*
Designer   Bernd Luz

12.
Client   *Honberg Sommer*
Designer   Bernd Luz

13.
Client   *Phillips Gallery of Fine Art*
Designer   Robert Wecker

14.
Client   *Stadt Geisingen*
Designer   Bernd Luz

15.
Client   *Colorado Dance Festival*
Designers   Jackson Boelts, Eric Boelts

1.

3TEX

2.

PROOF
OF CONCEPT

3.

Planworx

ARCHITECTURE, P.A.

4.

CSH

CRANFILL, SUMNER & HARTZOG, LLP

5.

6.

7.

Camp Jenney

The Camp For Kids With Cystic Fibrosis

8.

9.

10.

11.

12.

13.

14.

15.

1.

2.

3.

4.

5.

6.

7.

8.

water·color^{SM}

A Southern Coastal Landscape. **FLORIDA**

9.

10.

11.

12. A B A C U S

A|K F
e n g i n e e r s

13.

[J I V A C R E A T I V E]

14.

T E A M C A N A D A

15.

1 - 12
Design Firm **David Carter Design Associates**
13
Design Firm **Kristin Odermatt Design**
14
Design Firm **Jiva Creative**
15
Design Firm **McArthur Thompson & Law**

1.
Client *Disney Cruise Line*
Designer Emily Cain
Illustrator Dan Piraro
2.
Client *Mandalay Bay Resort*
Designer Tabitha Bogard
3.
Client *Mandalay Bay Resort*
Designer Tien Pham
4.
Client *Disney Cruise Line*
Designers Emily Cain, Jim Rucker
5.
Client *Mandalay Bay Resort*
Designer Kevin Prejean
6.
Client *Paris Casino Resort*
Designer Ashley Barron Mattocks
Illustrator Dan Piraro

7.
Client *Paris Casino Resort*
Designer Stephanie Pickering
8, 9.
Client *St. Joe/Arvida*
Designers Sharon LeJeune, Paul Munsterman
10.
Client *Walt Disney World*
Designer Tien Pham
11.
Client *Walt Disney World*
Designers Janet Davis, Rachel Graham
12.
Client *Abacus*
Designer Emily Cain
13.
Client *AKF Engineers*
Designers Kristin Odermatt, Deanna McClure
14.
Client *Jiva Creative*
Designer Eric Lee
15.
Client *Canadian National Snowboard Team*
Designer Michael Scher

1.

2.

3.

4.

SURETHOUGHT

5.

photosphere studio

6.

Spina Bifida
Association
of Dallas

7.

datamax

8.

kedestra

9.

10.

:10m design

11.

The Health & Wellness Center
BY DOYLESTOWN HOSPITAL

12.

EXHALE™

13.

SOMA FOUNDATION

14.

1, 4, 12
Design Firm **Art 270 Inc.**
2, 10
Design Firm **Bailey Design Group**
3, 13, 14
Design Firm **Artemis Creative, Inc.**
5, 7, 8
Design Firm **Griffith Phillips Creative**
6, 9, 11
Design Firm **BBK Studio**

1.
Client   *West German BMW*
Designer   Sean Flanagan
2.
Client   *Goldenberg Candy Company*
Designers   David Fiedler, Steve Perry,
           Denise Bosler
3.
Client   *Bio-Rad Laboratories/Pure Water*
Designers   Wes Aoki, Betsy Palay,
           Mark Gallo
Illustrators   Gary Nusinow,
           Lisa Turan
4.
Client   *West German BMW*
Designer   Sean Flanagan
5.
Client   *Surethought, www.surethought.com*
Designer   Brian Niemann

6.
Client   *Photosphere*
Designers   Sharon Oleniczak,
           Michele Chartier
7.
Client   *Spina Bifida Association of Dallas*
Designer   Bo McCord
8.
Client   *Datamax, www.datamax.com*
Designer   Brian Niemann
9.
Client   *Kedestra*
Designers   Yang Kim, Kelly J. Schwartz
10.
Client   *H.J. Heinz Co.*
Designers   David Fiedler, Gary LaCroix,
           Man Hong Ling
11.
Client   *Mike Boysen*
Designer   Sharon Oleniczak
12.
Client   *The Health and Wellness Center
           by Doylestown Hospital*
Designers   John Opet, Carl Mill
13.
Client   *Exhale Therapeutics, Inc.*
Designers   Betsy Palay, Jim Temple,
           Mark Gallo
14.
Client   *Soma Foundation*
Designers   Betsy Palay, Wes Aoki

1.

2.

3.

4.

5.

6.

7.

8.

9.

Travel Health Resource
expert world travel advice

10.

11.

 **Gazelle**

12.

Hearts and Hands
A CELEBRATION OF NEIGHBORS

13.

14.

CHINESE
INFORMATION
CENTRE

1.

2.

Premarin

SALTWATER CITY

3.

4. **POS** TOUCH SCREEN SYSTEMS

sesame
workshop™

5.

GREYSTONE

6.

THOUSAND WORDS

7.

AIRLUME
CANDLES

8.

9.

10.

a Contempo Design rental product

11.

12.

13.

14.

15.

1	Design Firm **ARTiculation Group**	4.	Client *Posera*
2	Design Firm **ARTiculation Group, PJDDB**		Designer Glenn Jansen
3, 4	Design Firm **Glenn Jansen Design**	5.	Client *Sesame Workshop*
5 - 7	Design Firm **Carbone Smolan Agency**		Designers K. Carbone, J. Peters, T. Sopkovich
8	Design Firm **Roger Christian & Co.**	6.	Client *Greystone*
9	Design Firm **Look Design**		Designers Ken Carbone, Justin Peters
10	Design Firm **Boyden & Youngblutt Advertising**	7.	Client *Thousand Words*
11	Design Firm **ZGraphics, Ltd.**		Designers Ken Carbone, Lesley Kunikis
12	Design Firm **Roka Inc.**	8.	Client *Airlume Candles*
13	Design Firm **Square Peg Graphics**		Designer Roger Christian
14	Design Firm **Resco Print Graphics**	9.	Client *Deli-Up Cafe*
15	Design Firm **Verizon—** **Corporate Multimedia Design**		Designers M. Schwedhelm, B. Todd, S. Jones
1.	Client *Chinese Information Centre*	10.	Client *Boyden & Youngblutt Advertising*
	Designer Joseph Chan		Designer Eric Cass
2.	Client *Wyeth Ayerst*	11.	Client *Contempo*
	Designer Joseph Chan		Designers Renee Clark, Joe Zeller
3.	Client *Saltwater City*	12.	Client *VIPhysique*
	Designer Glenn Jansen		Designer Karen DeMarino
		13.	Client *K&J Designs, Armoires Online*
			Designer Jack Jackson
		14.	Client *Babble-On Studios*
			Designer Sandy Plank
		15.	Client *AIANSS, Inc.*
			Designer Norbert Saez
			Illustrator Scott Harris

CALLISON

1.

COLUMBIA WINERY

2.

All-LASER

THE NEW EDGE

3.

Lawson Design

4.

HONDA
Care

5.

RIGHT *home*

6.

ProVide

ATTRACTING THE BEST

7.

RIVERWALK
VISTA

8.

9.

AT EASTWALK COMMONS

10.

NetAssets

11.

12.

Rufino®
candles

13.

14.

15.

1, 2
    Design Firm **Phinney/Bischoff Design House**
3, 4, 6
    Design Firm **Lawson Design**
5
    Design Firm **Rubin Postaer & Assoc.**
7, 8, 13
    Design Firm **Roger Christian & Co.**
9, 10
    Design Firm **Conover**
11
    Design Firm **Grafik Marketing Communications Ltd**
12
    Design Firm **Design Guys**
14
    Design Firm **Todd Nickel**
15
    Design Firm **Harbauer Bruce Nelson Design**

1.
    Client   *Callison Architecture*
    Designer   Dean Hart
2.
    Client   *Columbia Winery*
    Designer   Lorie Ransom
3.
    Client   *Intrasase*
    Designers   Jeff Lawson, Margaret Miyuki
4.
    Client   *Lawson Design*
    Designer   Jeff Lawson

5.
    Client   *Honda*
    Designer   Jeff Lawson
6.
    Client   *Right Home*
    Designer   Jeff Lawson
7.
    Client   *Aftermarket Auto Parts Alliance*
    Designer   Roger Christian
8.
    Client   *Riverwalk Vista*
    Designer   Roger Christian
9.
    Client   *Highway 101 Property Owners Association*
    Designers   David Conover, Damin Sterling
10.
    Client   *JMI Realty*
    Designers   David Conover, Damin Sterling
11.
    Client   *Net Assets*
    Designer   Michelle Mar
12.
    Client   *Sportevo*
    Designer   John Moes
13.
    Client   *Airlume Candles*
    Designer   Roger Christian
14.
    Client   *Sugar Beats*
    Designer   Todd Nickel
15.
    Client   *Sanford Corporation*
    Designer   Steve Walker

1.

2.

Strategic Engineering Initiatives

3.

4.

5.

6.

7.

8.

9.

10.

11.

wireless audio

12.

13.

beygl & barista
the bakery and coffee bar

14.

CAMPAGNE

French Country Cuisine

1.

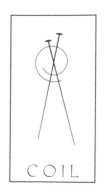

COIL

2.

3.

5.

6.

"squeak"

7.

8.

9.

10.

"meow"

SPIRIT SPORTS

11.

CATHOLIC
Archdiocese
O F   S T .   L O U I S

12.

MISS UNIVERSE 1983 ST. LOUIS U.S.A.

13.

14.

1, 2			
Design Firm **Kim Baer Design**		**4.**	
3		Client	*Dakota Halal Processing Company*
Design Firm **Michael Gunselman Incorporated**		Designers	Dixon & Parcels Associates, Inc.
4		**5.**	
Design Firm **Dixon & Parcels Associates, Inc.**		Client	*Stonewall Vineyards*
5		Designer	Barbara Brown
Design Firm **Barbara Brown**		**6.**	
Marketing & Design		Client	*Landlock*
6		Designer	Kelly Allen
Design Firm **Sullivan Perkins**		**7.**	
7, 10		Client	*Made on Earth Store*
Design Firm **Made on Earth**		Designer	Jay Vigon
8		**8.**	
Design Firm **Vaughn/Wedeen Creative**		Client	*USWest—The Heat is On*
9		Designer	Dan Flynn
Design Firm **Gunnar Swanson Design Office**		**9.**	
11 - 13		Client	*Gunnar Swanson Design Office*
Design Firm **McDermott Design**		Designer	Gunnar Swanson
14		**10.**	
Design Firm **Michael Lee Advertising &**		Client	*Made on Earth Store*
Design, Inc.		Designer	Jay Vigon
1.		**11.**	
Client	*Campagne*	Client	*Spirit Sports and Event Marketing*
Designer	Barbara Cooper	Designer	Bill McDermott
2.		**12.**	
Client	*Coil Knitwear*	Client	*Archdiocese of St. Louis*
Designers	Susan Landesmann, Kimberly Baer,	Designer	Bill McDermott
	Erin Ferro	**13.**	
3.		Client	*Miss Universe/*
Client	*Longwood Gardens*		*St. Louis Ambassadors*
Designer	Michael Gunselman	Designer	Bill McDermott
		14.	
		Client	*McFaddin-Ward House*
		Designer	Michael Lee

1.

2.

3.

4.

5.

6.

7.

8.

9.

10.

11.

12.

DROP
DEAD
ROCK

13.

14.

15.

1.

TOWERbank

2.

VISION &
mission

ONLINE
banking

COMMUNITY
connection

TOWERING
news

3.

4.

5.

6.

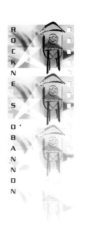

7.

wild
onion
CATERING

8.

HOLLYWOOD PHYSICAL THERAPY ASSOCIATES

9.

L X S

LEGEND SERIES
extreme

10.

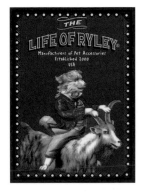

THE
LIFE OF RYLEY®
Manufacturers of Pet Accessories
Established 2000
USA

11.

just koz entertainment

12.

✕ TYSZNA ✕
GATUNEK
Q

13.

L A S
VEGAS

14.

15.

1 - 4, 10
   Design Firm **Boyden & Youngblutt Advertising**
5, 11, 15
   Design Firm **Wallace Church, Inc.**
6, 14
   Design Firm **Mires**
7, 9, 12
   Design Firm **Asylum**
8
   Design Firm **Delphine Keim Campbell**
13
   Design Firm **Parachute, Inc.**

1.
   Client   *Monark*
   Designers   Tim Favrote, Kelly Gayer
2.
   Client   *TowerBank*
   Designer   Jodi Matthias
3.
   Client   *TowerBank*
   Designer   Andy Boyden
4.
   Client   *MasterSpa*
   Designers   Chris Swymeler, Tim Favrote
5.
   Client   *Headline Productions*
   Designers   Wendy Church, Lucian Toma,
            Pat Lore

6.
   Client   *Big Deahl*
   Designers   Jose Serrano, Miguel Perez
7.
   Client   *Rockne O'Bannon*
   Designers   Andrea Wynnyk, Jim Shanman
8.
   Client   *Wild Onion Catering*
   Designer   Delphine Keim Campbell
9.
   Client   *Hollywood Physical Therapy Assoc.*
   Designers   Andrea Wynnyk, Jim Shanman
10.
   Client   *MasterSpa*
   Designers   Chris Swymeler, Tim Favrote
11.
   Client   *The Life of Ryley*
   Designers   Wendy Church, Michael Scaraglino
12.
   Client   *Just Koz Entertainment*
   Designers   Andrea Wynnyk, Jim Shanman
13.
   Client   *Millennium Import Co.*
   Designer   Heather Cooley
14.
   Client   *Las Vegas Chamber of Commerce*
   Designers   Jose Serrano, Miguel Perez
15.
   Client   *Wallace Church, Inc.*
   Designers   Stan Church, Nin Glaister,
            Lawrence Haggerty

1.

2.

3.

4.

5.

6.

7.

8.

9.

LEAP™

10.

BRETON
BANVILLE
& ASSOCIÉS

11.

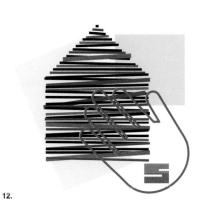

12.

Leger
MARKETING

13.

PASTA INDUSTRIES

14.

The TURN
SNACK BAR

15.

1 - 3
　Design Firm **Interflow Communications Ltd.**
4, 5, 7, 8, 14, 15
　Design Firm **Lidia Varesco Design**
6, 9, 12
　Design Firm **Bruce Yelaska Design**
10
　Design Firm **Addison**
11, 13
　Design Firm **Vasco Design**
1.
　Client　　　*Area 51*
2.
　Client　　　*CPC Rafhan*
3.
　Client　　　*Young Presidents' Organization*
4.
　Client　　　*Levy Restaurants/*
　　　　　　　Indian Lakes Resort
5.
　Client　　　*Shutterbug Studios*
　Designer　　Lidia Varesco
6.
　Client　　　*Saarman Construction*
　Designer　　Bruce Yelaska

7.
　Client　　　*Levy Restaurants/*
　　　　　　　Indian Lakes Resort
　Designer　　Lidia Varesco
8.
　Client　　　*Levy Restaurants/Bistro Toujours*
　Designer　　Lidia Varesco
9.
　Client　　　*Saarman Construction*
　Designer　　Bruce Yelaska
10.
　Client　　　*Leap*
　Designers　　Robin Awes, David Schuemann
11.
　Client　　　*BBA Engineers*
　Designers　　Francine Léger, Vasco Ceccon
12.
　Client　　　*Saarman Construction*
　Designer　　Bruce Yelaska
13.
　Client　　　*Leger Marketing*
　Designer　　Francine Leger
14.
　Client　　　*Pasta Industries*
　Designer　　Lidia Varesco
15.
　Client　　　*Levy Restaurants/*
　　　　　　　Indian Lakes Resort
　Designer　　Lidia Varesco

1.

2.

3.

4.

5.

6.

7

8.

BRIGHTON AVENUE

9.

ca$h zone

10.

Domino's Pizza *Italian Originals*™

11.

S.M.A.R.T

12.

GRiLL & *glaze*

13.

JIMMY AND DOUG'S
FC
FARMCLUB.COM

14.

15.

1.

2.

3.

4.

Caffé
ANTICOLI

5.

CLAYBURNE PLACE

6.

miamivalleycentremall
The centre of your life.

7.

8.

226

WEST RIDGE
CHURCH

9.

virtualteams.com

10.

11.

12.

LORD BISSELL ⬦ BROOK
ATTORNEYS AT LAW

13.

Monroe Federal
Defining Local Banking

14.

1, 2, 13
Design Firm **Greenfield Belser Ltd.**
3, 6, 12
Design Firm **WorldSTAR Design**
4, 8, 10, 11
Design Firm **Gill Fishman Associates**
5, 7, 14
Design Firm **1-earth GRAPHICS**
9
Design Firm **Greg Guhl**

1.
Client — *In2Books*
Designer — Janet Morales
2.
Client — *Orrick Herrington & Sutcliffe*
Designer — Stephanie Fernandez
3.
Client — *Georgia Hospital Association*
Designer — Greg Guhl
4.
Client — *Entercept*
Designers — Gill Fishman, Alicia Ozyjowski
5.
Client — *Caffé Anticoli*
Designer — David Radabaugh

6.
Client — *Clayburne Place*
Designer — Greg Guhl
7.
Client — *Miami Valley Center Mall*
Designer — Lisa Harris
8.
Client — *Edgewing/Plant Consulting*
Designers — Gill Fishman, Michael Persons
9.
Client — *West Ridge Church*
Designer — Greg Guhl
10.
Client — *Virtual Teams/Netage*
Designers — Gill Fishman, Alicia Ozyjowski
11.
Client — *Variagenics*
Designers — Gill Fishman, Michael Persons
12.
Client — *Offset Atlanta, Inc.*
Designer — Greg Guhl
13.
Client — *Lord Bissell Brook*
Designers — John Bruns, Tom Cameron
14.
Client — *Monroe Federal*
Designer — Lisa Harris

3.

1.

Alphafuels

2.

4.

5.

6.

7.

8.

9.

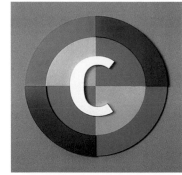

10.

11.

2000
healthworld
ENTREPRENEURIAL FORUM

12.

capps
digital studio

13.

EMPIRE THEATRES

Entertainment.
We Set The Stage.

14.

1, 6
Design Firm **Primo Angeli Inc.**
2, 7
Design Firm **Kirby Stephens Design**
3
Design Firm **Miravo Communications**
4
Design Firm **Blöch + Coulter Design Group**
5
Design Firm **EGO Design**
8
Design Firm **Hornall Anderson Design Works**
9, 12, 14
Design Firm **McArthur Thompson & Law**
10, 11, 13
Design Firm **Leo Burnett**
1.
Client   *Church's Chicken*
Designers   Ariel Villasol, Peter Matsukawa,
             Kelson Mau
2.
Client   *Autoindulgence*
3.
Client   *Glofrog*
Designer   Justan Lustan
4.
Client   *Blöch + Coulter Design Group*
Designer   Ellie Young Suh

5.
Client   *EGO Design*
Designer   George Otvos
6.
Client   *Saraide*
Designer   Ariel Villasol
7.
Client   *Autoindulgence*
8.
Client   *Twelve Horses*
Designers   Jack Anderson, Lisa Cerveny,
             Mary Chin Hutchison, Don Stayner
9.
Client   *Sweet Jane's*
Designers   Rob Hansen, Jay Silver
10, 13.
Client   *Capps Digital Studio*
Designers   Linda Goldberg, James Murphy
11.
Client   *Gene Siskel Film Center*
Designers   Linda Goldberg, Jim Wood
12.
Client   *Healthworld*
Designer   Rob Hansen
14.
Client   *Empire Theatres*
Designer   Min Landry

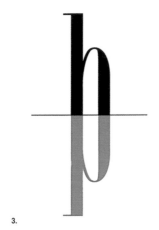

1.

2.

3.

4.

5.

6.

7.

Primizie

8.

9.

project sunshine
bringing sunshine to a cloudy day℠

10.

take lead!
Step into the light
the

11.

88
Sr

12.

13.

14.

15.

1.

2.

3.

4.

Advanced Medicine

5.

6.

7.

8.

232

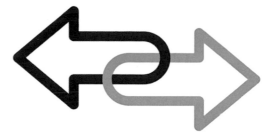

9.

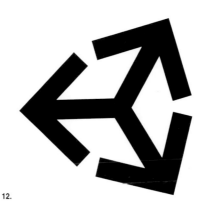

10.

11.

12.

MILLER'S MILLWORKS

13.

TELSEON

14.

TETRAGON

15.

1.

HEAD SOCKET

2.

first line ™

3.

DOUBLETAKES

4.

nutriance

5.

CITY
secrets
Rome

6.

pirate net

7.

MARSHFIELD CLINIC

8.

[vir2oso]

THE ART of COOKING

9.

PhotoPoint
.com

10.

12.

11. RECHARGE

13.

14.

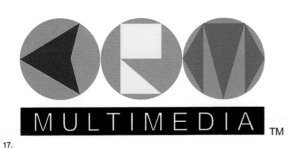

15.

MILLENNIUM

16.

MULTIMEDIA™

17.

1.

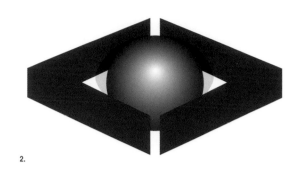

2.

3.

4.

5.

6.

7

8.

DigitalMOBILESOLUTION

9.

10.

V I C T O R I A

S Y M P H O N Y

11.

Carmanah

12.

THE CITY OF
VICTORIA

13.

14.

PURDUE INTERNATIONAL CENTER FOR
ENTERTAINMENT TECHNOLOGY

15.

1, 5, 7, 8, 10 - 13
Design Firm **Trapeze Communications**
2 - 4, 6, 9, 14
Design Firm **Pete Smith Design**
15
Design Firm **Purdue University**

1.
Client   *Government Agents*
Designer   Mark Bawden
2.
Client   *Virtual Visit Presentations*
Designer   Pete Smith
3.
Client   *Design in Motion*
Designer   Pete Smith
4.
Client   *Venture Assistants*
Designer   Pete Smith
5.
Client   *Unity*
Designer   Mark Bawden
6.
Client   *Traffic Lite*
Designer   Pete Smith
7.
Client   *Art Gallery of Greater Victoria*
Designer   Mark Bawden

8.
Client   *BC's Family Fishing Weekend*
Designer   Mark Bawden
9.
Client   *Digital Mobile Solution*
Designer   Pete Smith
10.
Client   *Ministry of Women's Equality*
Designer   Mark Bawden
11.
Client   *Victoria Symphony*
Designer   Mark Bawden
12.
Client   *Carmanah Technologies*
Designer   Mark Bawden
13.
Client   *City of Victoria*
Designer   Mark Bawden
14.
Client   *Praxisoft*
Designer   Pete Smith
15.
Client   *Purdue International Center for
Entertainment Technology*
Designer   Li Zhang

1.

SANDIE JACOBS & ASSOCIATES

2.

3.

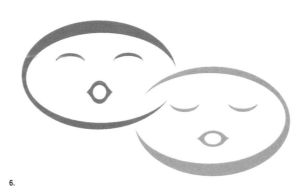

4.

5.

6.

7.

8.

9.

10.

11.

First
Baptist
Church
1799-1999

12.

13.

14.

15.

1		
	Design Firm	**Boyden & Youngblutt Advertising**
2		
	Design Firm	**Hiroshi Hamada Design Studio**
3 - 5, 8, 9, 11, 12		
	Design Firm	**Kirby Stephens Design**
6, 10, 13 - 15		
	Design Firm	**Shea**
7		
	Design Firm	**Wittwer Industries**
1.		
	Client	*Lincoln Re Insurance*
	Designers	Andy Boyden, Tim Favrote
2.		
	Client	*Sandie Jacobs & Associates*
	Designer	Hiroshi Hamada
3.		
	Client	*KY Guild of Artists & Craftsmen*
4.		
	Client	*The Center for Rural Development*
5.		
	Client	*Sumerset Houseboats*
6.		
	Client	*Ooh Aah*
	Designer	Pam McFerrin

7.		
	Client	*Kil Karney Mist*
	Designer	Jason Wittwer
8.		
	Client	*Sumerset Houseboats*
9.		
	Client	*Bastin's Steakhouse*
10.		
	Client	*Marshall Field's—Mixed Greens*
	Designer	Holly Utech
11.		
	Client	*East Kentucky Network*
12.		
	Client	*First Baptist Church*
13.		
	Client	*Select Comfort—Retail Store*
	Designer	James Rahn
14.		
	Client	*Shea, Inc.*
	Designers	Eric Fetrow, Viera Hartmannova
15.		
	Client	*Toys 'R' Us*
	Designers	James Rahn, Jason Wittwer

1.

2.

AlphaLeader

3.

4.

5.

6.

7.

8.

VANTAGE
EYE CENTER

9.

APEX
SIGNS & GRAPHICS

10.

11.

12.

13.

MILESTONE
CONSTRUCTION MANAGEMENT

14.

15.

1.

2.

3.

Monte Vista
small animal hospital

4.

5.

corporate kids

6.

sportstyle

7.

8.

HEALTHY START
MODESTO CITY SCHOOLS

9.

HAFERS
HOME FURNISHINGS

10.

CENTRAL VALLEY IMAGING ASSOCIATES

11.

ACADEMY OF INFORMATION TECHNOLOGY

12.

RHODE ISLAND INTERLOCAL
The Trust
RISK MANAGEMENT TRUST

13.

ARMADANI

14.

15.

1.

2.

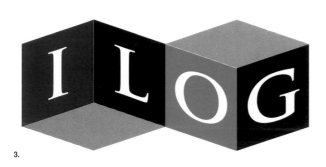

3.

4.

5.

6.

7.

8.

9.

10.

11.

12.

Hulingshof

13.

14.

15.

1
   Design Firm **FRCH Design Worldwide (Cincinnati)**
2, 3, 12
   Design Firm **Landkamer Partners**
4
   Design Firm **Wet Paper Bag Graphic Design**
5 - 11, 13 - 15
   Design Firm **Buttgereit und Heidenreich**

1.
   Client   *Bostonian*
   Designers   Mike Brod, Dawn Wolf
2.
   Client   *Commerce One*
   Designers   Mark Landkamer, Gene Clark
3.
   Client   *ILOG*
   Designers   Mark Landkamer, Gene Clark
4.
   Client   *Texas Christian University Journalism Department*
   Designer   Lewis Glaser
5.
   Client   *C2 Team Coaching*
   Designer   Michael Buttgereit
6.
   Client   *Team. F*
   Designers   Michael Buttgereit, Karsten Kordus
7.
   Client   *VNR Verlag*
   Designers   Michael Buttgereit, Wolfram Heidenreich

8.
   Client   *ERF Evangeliumsrundfunk*
   Designers   Michael Buttgereit, Wolfram Heidenreich
9.
   Client   *Hoffnungszeichen (Sign of Hope)*
   Designers   Michael Buttgereit, Wolfram Heidenreich
10.
   Client   *Siebter Kontinent Interaktive Medien*
   Designer   Michael Buttgereit
11.
   Client   *Lindner*
   Designers   Michael Buttgereit, Wolfram Heidenreich
12.
   Client   *Nuance*
   Designers   Mark Landkamer, Gene Clark
13.
   Client   *Hulingshof*
   Designer   Wolfram Heidenreich
14.
   Client   *Simplify your Life*
   Designers   Michael Buttgereit, Wolfram Heidenreich
15.
   Client   *Innovo AG*
   Designers   Michael Buttgereit, Wolfram Heidenreich

1.

2.

3.

4.

5.

6.

7.

8.

9.

TruSpeed MotorCars™
Specializing in Exotic and Collectible Auto Sales

10.

It's About Speed

11.

12.

13.

uNetC•MMERCE™
UNIFIED INTERNET COMMERCE

14.

15.

1.

P H O E N I X

2.

CHILDREN'S HOME SOCIETY OF NORTH CAROLINA. EST. 1902

L I T T L E   R E D   S T O C K I N G   F U N D

3.

4.

GREENSBORO
RADIOLOGY
THE MEDICAL IMAGING PROFESSIONALS

5.

JUDGES | STAFFING | GROUP

Visionaries With Solutions

6.

THE
DESIGN
GROUP

INTEGRATED

MARKETING

COMMUNICATIONS

7.

GRAPHIC SYSTEMS
I N T E R N A T I O N A L

8.

F E A R R I N G T O N
village

9.

W o r k S m a r t

10.

from **HEAD** *to* **TOE**

11.

12.

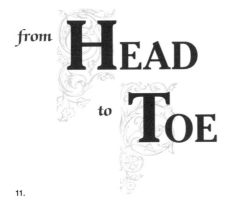

LEXINGTON ANESTHESIA

13.

ENVIRONMENTS
a studio for home and garden

14.

INMARK

FURNITURE

15.

1.

2.

3.

4.

5.

6.

7.

8.

9.

ABINGTON
ART CENTER

10.

11.

D O R S Á L

12.

Old Tennent
Presbyterian Church
— founded in 1692 —

13.

14.

15.

White Hen

1.

INTERFACE

C H I L D R E N
F A M I L Y
S E R V I C E S

2.

Quantum**Shift**™

3.

KUMAI HARVEST™

4.

H Y O S H I N

5.

C Y N T R I C

6.

k i n e c t a ™

7.

The
Learning Community
I N S T I T U T E S

8.

Anchor Education

9.

10.

iospan
wireless™

11.

KICKFIRE™

12.

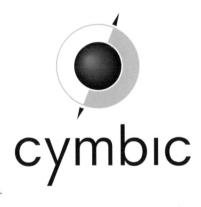
cymbic

13.

Z H O N E

14.

15.

1
Design Firm **Addison**
2, 8, 9, 15
Design Firm **Barbara Brown**
Marketing & Design
3 - 7, 10 - 14
Design Firm **Cymbic**

1.
Client   *Clark Retail Enterprises:*
          White Hen Pantry
Designers David Schuemann, Lisa Schuemann

2.
Client   *Interface*
Designer Barbara Brown

3.
Client   *Quantum Shift*
Designers Kénichi Nishiwaki, Ken Kubo,
          Yong An, David Nicol

4.
Client   *Kumai Harvest*
Designers Kénichi Nishiwaki, Michael Fu-Ming,
          Amanda Ely, Joanna Dolby

5.
Client   *Hyogo Shinkin Bank*
Designers Kénichi Nishiwaki, Ken Kubo,
          Ronald Blodgett

6.
Client   *Cyntric*
Designers Kénichi Nishiwaki, Amanda Ely,
          Ken Kubo, Yong An

7.
Client   *Kinecta*
Designers Kénichi Nishiwaki, Scott Jackson,
          Tracy Christensen

8.
Client   *TLCI*
Designer Barbara Brown

9.
Client   *Anchor Education*
Designer Barbara Brown

10.
Client   *Nutiva*
Designers Kénichi Nishiwaki, Michael Fu-Ming

11.
Client   *Iospan Wireless*
Designers Kénichi Nishiwaki, Ken Kubo,
          Yong An, Ronald Blodgett

12.
Client   *Kickfire*
Designers Kénichi Nishiwaki, Ken Kubo,
          Ronald Blodgett

13.
Client   *Cymbic*
Designers Kénichi Nishiwaki, Amanda Ely,
          Joanna Dolby, Michael Fu-Ming

14.
Client   *Zhone Technologies*
Designers Kénichi Nishiwaki, Joanna Dolby,
          Amanda Ely, Michael Fu-Ming

15.
Client   *Ronald Reagan*
          Presidential Foundation
Designers Barbara Brown, Amy Schneider,
          Jon A. Leslie

1. WIDE IDEA

THINK FASTER
THINK XEROX

2.

enfish.
One space

3.

FALBROOKE
AT KRISTOPHER RANCH
SHEAHOMES

4.

THINK FASTER
THINK XEROX

X

5.

the **Kiln**
Doctor Inc.

6.

newpak

U S A

7.

CORK
SUPPLY
GROUP

8.

9.

10.

11.

THEMSWALK

12.

13.

SIXMAN**IAC.**

14.

15.

1.

2.

HALF MOON BAY
PUMPKIN RUN

OCTOBER 14, 2001

3.

TEXERE

4.

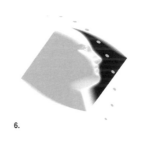

5.

6.

7.

8.

9.

10.

11.

12.

13.

14.

15.

1, 7, 9, 12, 13
Design Firm **The Benchmark Group**
2, 5, 6, 10, 14
Design Firm **Berni Marketing & Design**
3, 4, 8, 11, 15
Design Firm **Mastandrea Design, Inc.**

1.
Client   *Cincinnati Ballet*
Designer   John Carpenter

2.
Client   *Biscotti & Co.*
Designer   Carlos Seminario

3.
Client   *Half Moon Bay Pumpkin Run/*
         Senior Coast Siders
Designer   Mary Anne Mastandrea

4.
Client   *Texere*
Designer   Mary Anne Mastandrea

5.
Client   *Biscotti & Co.*
Designer   Carlos Seminario

6.
Client   *Berni Marketing & Design*
Designer   Carlos Seminario

7.
Client   *Cincinnati Ballet*
Designers   John Carpenter, Jen O'Shea
Illustrator   Ken Meade

8.
Client   *U.S.Advisor*
Designer   Mary Anne Mastandrea

9.
Client   *Cincinnati Ballet*
Designers   John Carpenter, Jen O'Shea
Illustrator   Ken Meade

10.
Client   *Acappella*
Designer   Peter Antipas

11.
Client   *Creagri, LLC*
Designer   Mary Anne Mastandrea

12.
Client   *Oil of Olay*
Designer   John Carpenter
Illustrator   Ken Meade

13.
Client   *Cincinnati Ballet*
Designers   John Carpenter, Jen O'Shea
Illustrator   Ken Meade

14.
Client   *Castleberry Snows*

15.
Client   *Get Real Girl, Inc.*
Designer   Mary Anne Mastandrea

1.

2.

3.

4.

5.

6.

7.

8.

9.

10. IAAPA

11.

12.

Digital Acorns, Inc.
Growing the Business of Technology
13.

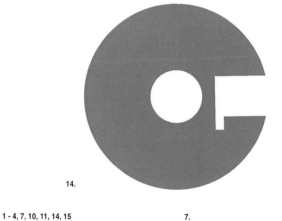

14.

15.

1 - 4, 7, 10, 11, 14, 15
  Design Firm **Kircher, Inc.**
5, 9, 12, 13
  Design Firm **Vance Wright Adams & Associates**
6
  Design Firm **Art 270, Inc.**
8
  Design Firm **Dixon & Parcels Associates, Inc.**

1.
  Client   *Kids After School*
  Designer   Bruce E. Morgan
2.
  Client   *American Chemical Society*
  Designer   Ben Straka
3.
  Client   *American Chemical Society*
  Designers   Bruce E. Morgan, Ben Straka, John Frantz
4.
  Client   *Food Marketing Institute*
  Designer   Bruce E. Morgan
5.
  Client   *Rick John Inc.*
  Designers   Vance Wright Adams and Associates
6.
  Client   *Art 270, Inc.*
  Designer   Steve Kuttruff

7.
  Client   *SkyRocketer*
  Designer   Bruce E. Morgan
8.
  Client   *Winn-Dixie Stores, Inc.*
  Designers   Dixon & Parcels Associates, Inc.
9.
  Client   *Ben Franklin Technology Partners*
  Designers   Vance Wright Adams and Associates
10.
  Client   *International Association of Amusement Parks and Attractions*
  Designer   Bruce E. Morgan
11.
  Client   *Satellite Broadcasting & Communications Association*
  Designer   Ben Straka
12.
  Client   *E-Promotions Inc.*
  Designers   Vance Wright Adams and Associates
13.
  Client   *Digital Acorns, Inc.*
  Designers   Vance Wright Adams and Associates
14.
  Client   *Concept Interactive, Inc.*
  Designer   Bruce E. Morgan
15.
  Client   *National Assoc. of Home Builders*
  Designer   Bruce E. Morgan

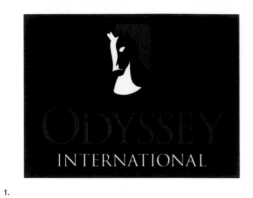

1.

2.

3.

4.

5.

6.

7.

8.

PROFESSIONAL SMILE SALON
First Impressions™

9.

HIXSON

10.

USTA
UNITED STATES
TELECOM
ASSOCIATION

11.

Federal Highway Administration
Office of Policy

12.

VentureForth

13.

L I F E S C A N

14.

b4bpartner

15.

1, 4, 5, 8, 11 - 13
 Design Firm **Sparkman + Associates**
2, 3, 6, 10, 14, 15
 Design Firm **Gouthier Design, Inc.**
7
 Design Firm **Greteman Group**
9
 Design Firm **GOLD & Associates**

1.
 Client   *Odyssey International*
 Designer   Ryan Weible
2.
 Client   *Paramount Hotel Group*
 Designer   Jonathan Gouthier
3.
 Client   *Grapevine Gourmet*
 Designers   Jonathan Gouthier, Katerina Nadel
4.
 Client   *Aprize Satellite*
 Designer   Don Sparkman
5.
 Client   *Blake Real Estate, Inc.*
 Designers   Don Sparkman, Melanie Wilkins
6.
 Client   *Elemental Solutions, Inc.*
 Designers   Jonathan Gouthier, Marina
             Fagerstrom, Katerina Nadel

7.
 Client   *ConnectCare*
 Designers   Sonia Greteman, James Strange
8.
 Client   *Goodwill Communications*
 Designer   Don Sparkman
9.
 Client   *First Impressions*
 Designers   Keith Gold, Rob McFarland
10.
 Client   *Hixson*
 Designer   Jonathan Gouthier
11.
 Client   *United States Telecom Association*
 Designer   Don Sparkman
12.
 Client   *Federal Highway Administration*
 Designer   Don Sparkman
13.
 Client   *VentureForth*
 Designer   Don Sparkman
14.
 Client   *Lifescan*
 Designer   Jonathan Gouthier
15.
 Client   *B4B Partner*
 Designer   Jonathan Gouthier

1.

2.

waterpik

3.

A B A C U S

4.

EKCO®

5.

VIGILANCE

6.

ARTISAN
PROFESSIONAL COOKWARE

7.

8.

Exactly!

9.

10.

11.

12.

newmoon·com

13.

mudd®

14.

15.

1 - 3, 5, 7, 12, 14, 15
Design Firm **Source/Inc.**
4, 6, 8 - 11, 13
Design Firm **Mark Selfe Design**

1.
Client   Kraft Foods, Inc.
2.
Client   Brunswick Recreation Group
3.
Client   Waterpik Technologies
4.
Client   Abacus Jewelry
Designer Mark Selfe
5.
Client   World Kitchen
6.
Client   Vigilance
Designer Mark Selfe
7.
Client   Mirro Wearever

8.
Client   Glorietta Elementary School
Designer Mark Selfe
9.
Client   Exactly Vertical
Designer Mark Selfe
10.
Client   Hatcher Press
Designer Mark Selfe
11.
Client   Eurstyle.com
Designer Mark Selfe
12.
Client   Nacional de Chocolates, S.A.
13.
Client   NewMoon.com
Designer Mark Selfe
14.
Client   Chattem, Inc. Consumer Products
15.
Client   Valeo, Inc.

1. solomiO

2.

3.

4. WHITEBOX advisors

5.  Give2Asia

6.  NEWGROUND

7.

8.

9.

10.

Think outside.

11.

WallaWare

12.

FreshSeal™

13.

peoplebusinessnetwork™

People working better.

14.

15.

1, 2, 6, 7
Design Firm **Mortensen Design**
3
Design Firm **Funk & Associates**
4
Design Firm **Tilka Design**
5
Design Firm **Fifth Street Design**
8
Design Firm **Zunda Design Group**
9, 13
Design Firm **Bailey Design Group**
10, 12, 14
Design Firm **The People Business Network**
11, 15
Design Firm **Wilmer Fong + Associates**

1.
Client   *Solomio*
Designer   Michael McDaniel
2.
Client   *Futurus Bank*
Designers   P.J. Nidecker, Wendy Chon,
          Gordon Mortensen
3.
Client   *Wet Dawg*
Designer   Beverly Soasey
4.
Client   *Whitebox advisors*
Designer   Shannon Shriver
5.
Client   *Give2Asia*
Designers   J. Clifton Meek, Brenton Beck

6.
Client   *Newground Resources*
Designer   P.J. Nidecker
7.
Client   *MyTalk, Inc.*
Designer   P.J. Nidecker
8.
Client   *B+G Foods, Inc.*
Designers   Todd Nickel, Charles Zunda
9.
Client   *Dechert*
Designers   David Fiedler, Gary LaCroix
10.
Client   *Verizon Wireless*
Designer   Ken Thorlton
11.
Client   *Wilmer Fong + Associates*
Designer   Kean Hiroshima
12.
Client   *WallaWare, Inc.*
Designer   David Pfeiffer
13.
Client   *CPG Technologies*
Designers   David Fiedler, Ken Cahill,
          Ann Marie Malone
14.
Client   *The People Business Network*
Designer   Ken Thorlton
15.
Client   *Pleasanton Girls Soccer Association*
Designers   Steve Jeong, Nina Edwards

1.

2. EPOS | endless possibilites productions inc.

3.

design

4.

5.

6.

songwriter records

7.

8.

9. **Concept** Laboratories, Inc.

10. PIZZA COMPANY

year up

11.

12. CLINIG·EN

north
shore
swimwear

13.

aloha
swimwear

14.

1, 2
Design Firm **EPOS, Inc.**
3 - 14
Design Firm **What! design**

1.
  Client   *EPOS Concepts, Inc.*
  Designer Clifford Singontiko

2.
  Client   *EPOS, Inc.*
  Designer Clifford Singontiko

3.
  Client   *Bank Capital*
  Designers Damon Meibers, George Restrepo

4.
  Client   *L2P Design*
  Designers Damon Meibers, Amy Strauch

5.
  Client   *Clearcut Recording*
  Designer Damon Meibers

6.
  Client   *Indy Girl*
  Designers Damon Meibers,
               Aaron Carmisciano,
               George Restrepo, Derek Aylward

7.
  Client   *Songwriter Records*
  Designers Damon Meibers, Derek Aylward

8.
  Client   *pmSolutions*
  Designer Damon Meibers

9.
  Client   *Concept Laboratories, Inc.*
  Designer Damon Meibers

10.
  Client   *Crazy Dough's Pizza Company*
  Designers Damon Meibers, Aaron Carmisciano

11.
  Client   *Year Up*
  Designers Damon Meibers, Aaron Carmisciano

12.
  Client   *Clinigen Inc.*
  Designers Damon Meibers, George Restrepo

13.
  Client   *North Shore Swimwear*
  Designers Damon Meibers, Derek Aylward

14.
  Client   *North Shore Swimwear—*
               Aloha Swimwear
  Designers Damon Meibers, Derek Aylward

1.

2.

3.

The
adventure
program

4.

5.

6.

7.

8.

MAUZY
Management, inc.

9.

Tac's
P L A C E

10.

SO!

11.

STRATEGIC CHANGE MANAGEMENT

13.

NEW CHALLENGES **YEAR 2000** NEW OPPORTUNITIES

14.

1.

2.

adah oaks angus

3.

4.

5.

6.

7.

8.

9.

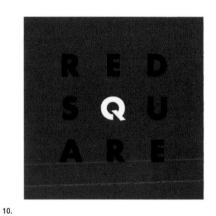

10.

11.

MARQUIS
HOSPITALITY GROUP

12.

SOUTHEAST
MUTUAL INSURANCE
C O M P A N Y

13.

1 - 4, 6 - 9, 11 - 13
Design Firm **Sign Here, Inc.**
5, 10
Design Firm **Landesberg Design Associates**

1.
Client *Rockhound Trucking*
Designer Melissa Shea

2.
Client *Rochester Floral & Gifts*
Designer Melissa Shea

3.
Client *Adah Oaks Angus*
Designer Lori Reynolds

4.
Client *Andy's Deli (Chafoulias Companies)*
Designer Lori Reynolds

5.
Client *City Theatre*
Designers Rick Landesberg, Joe Petrina

6.
Client *Blazing Needles*
Designer Lori Reynolds

7.
Client *Amish Furniture Barn*
Designer Melissa Shea

8.
Client *Frost Painting & Taping*
Designer Lori Reynolds

9.
Client *Hamilton Builders*
Designer Melissa Shea

10.
Client *Red Square Systems*
Designers Rick Landesberg, Vicki Carlisle,
Joe Petrina, Mike Savitski

11.
Client *Go-Fer Delivery
(Rochester Transportation Systems)*
Designer Lori Reynolds

12.
Client *Marquis Hospitality Group
(Chafoulias Companies)*
Designer Lori Reynolds

13.
Client *Southeast Mutual Insurance*
Designer Melissa Shea

1.

Carleton

2.

newmediary·com

3.

4.

eCopy™

5.

6.

7.

eau

8.

9.

10.

MY

FIVE STAR

CHEF

11.

D O R F

C A F É

12.

Contour Genesis®
Ultrasonic Surgery System

13.

S

14.

MECHWERKS

MECHWERKS

15.

1.

2.

3.

4.

5.

6.

7.

8.

Sunnyhill
A D V E N T U R E S

9.

10.

Camp
MarCom
Fleishman-Hillard
2000

11.

12.

NEW YORK URBAN LEAGUE

13.

ST. LOUIS
BLUES
NATIONAL HOCKEY LEAGUE
Established 1967

14.

BlueBolt
NETWORKS

15.

1 - 14
Design Firm **Fleishman-Hillard Creative**
15
Design Firm **Alexander Isley Inc.**
1.
Client   *St. Louis Blues*
Designer Buck Smith
2.
Client   *The Argent Hotel*
Designers Kevin Kampwerth, Paul Scherfling
3.
Client   *Biomedical Systems, Inc.*
Designer Kevin Kampwerth
4.
Client   *Fleishman-Hillard*
Designer Buck Smith
5.
Client   *SBC Communications, Inc.*
Designer Buck Smith
6.
Client   *Fleishman-Hillard*
Designer Mike Montandon
7.
Client   *Washington Monarch Hotel*
Designer Susan Gillham

8.
Client   *St. Louis Blues*
Designer Buck Smith
9.
Client   *Sunnyhill Adventures*
Designers John Senseney, Kevin Kampwerth
10.
Client   *San Francisco Giants*
Designer Buck Smith
11.
Client   *Fleishman-Hillard*
Designer Vicky Ho
12.
Client   *Hazelwood Central High School*
Designer Buck Smith
13.
Client   *New York Urban League*
Designer Ed Mantels-Seeker
14.
Client   *St. Louis Blues*
Designer Buck Smith
15.
Client   *Bluebolt Networks*
Designers Alexander Isley, Liesl Kaplan

PrimoGifts

1.

THE COPLEY
CONDOMINIUM AND CLUB

2.

Tacoma
wine classic

3.

eClips Now
video
for
the
www

4.

JEWISH ORTHODOX FEMINIST ALLIANCE

jofa

5.

THE TAX STORE

6.

A Secret Garden

7.

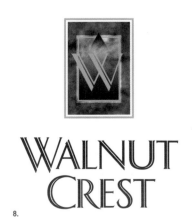

WALNUT CREST

8.

9.

10.

11.

12.

13.

14.

15.

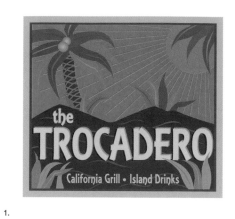

1.

2.

3.

4.

5.

6.

7.

8.

9.

10.

11.

12.

13.

14.

15.

(all)
Design Firm **On the Edge Design**

1.
Client   *The Trocadero*
Designers   Jeff Gasper, Gina Mims

2.
Client   *Blu Water Cafe*
Designers   Jeff Gasper, Tracey Lamberson

3.
Client   *Jillian's—Hi Life Lanes*
Designers   Jeff Gasper, Gina Mims

4.
Client   *L'Opera*
Designers   Jeff Gasper, Nicole Geiger-Brown

5.
Client   *Platinum*
Designers   Jeff Gasper, Nicole Geiger-Brown

6.
Client   *Mesquite Beach*
Designers   Jeff Gasper, Scott Jackson

7.
Client   *JT Schmids*
Designers   Jeff Gasper, Gina Mims

8.
Client   *Jillian's*
Designers   Jeff Gasper, Gina Mims

9.
Client   *French 75*
Designers   Jeff Gasper, Gina Mims

10.
Client   *Sea Grill*
Designers   Jeff Gasper, Nicole Geiger-Brown

11.
Client   *Johns Incredible Pizza*
Designers   Jeff Gasper, Nicole Geiger-Brown

12.
Client   *Caffee Panini*
Designers   Jeff Gasper, Nicole Geiger-Brown

13.
Client   *Green Epstein Bacino*
Designers   Jeff Gasper, Nicole Geiger-Brown

14.
Client   *BlueCat Cafe*
Designers   Jeff Gasper, Gina Mims

15.
Client   *Sonomas Grill*
Designers   Jeff Gasper, Tracey Lamberson

PORTICO

CHERRY CREEK

1.

SETTINGS™

CASUAL HOME FURNISHINGS

2.

0.05 design

3.

TOOLS FOR LIVING

4.

HAVERHILL

PUBLIC LIBRARY

5.

MOA

MUSEUM
OF OUTDOOR
ARTS

6.

BEL MAR

A GREAT LOCATION

NEVER GOES OUT OF STYLE.

7.

THE
MASTER'S
PROGRAM

8.

9.

10.

11.

12.

13.

KELLY, SC☾TT & MADISON

14.

15.

1, 3, 6, 7
Design Firm **Ellen Bruss Design**
2, 4, 5
Design Firm **Primary Design, Inc.**
8
Design Firm **McAdams Group**
9, 11
Design Firm **Funk & Associates**
10, 14
Design Firm **JOED Design Inc.**
12
Design Firm **Laura Manthey Design**
13
Design Firm **FRCH Design Worldwide**
(Cincinnati)
15
Design Firm **Defteling Design**

1.
Client   *Kestrel Partners*
Designers   Ellen Bruss, Charles Carpenter
2.
Client   *Settings*
Designers   Allison Davis, Jules Epstein
3.
Client   *zero.zero five design*
Designer   Ellen Bruss
4.
Client   *Tools for Living*
Designers   Kristen Lossman, Jules Epstein
5.
Client   *Haverhill Public Library*
Designers   Jasmine Gillingham, Jules Epstein

6.
Client   *Museum of Outdoor Arts*
Designers   Ellen Bruss, Charles Carpenter,
            Daryll Peirce, Kara Cullen
7.
Client   *Continuum Partners*
Designers   Ellen Bruss, Charles Carpenter
8.
Client   *The Master's Program*
Designers   Larry McAdams, Michael Paff
9.
Client   *eBridge*
Designers   Chris Berner, David Funk
10.
Client   *Infant Welfare Society of Chicago*
Designer   Tim Pressley
11.
Client   *Kelly King & Associates*
Designer   Alex Wijnen
12.
Client   *The Mad Catter*
Designer   Laura Manthey
13.
Client   *Tempus Entertainment*
Designer   Juliet Fierer
14.
Client   *Kelly Scott & Madison*
Designer   Charisse McAloon
15.
Client   *Paradise Media*
Designer   Alex Wijnen

281

1.

2.

3.

4.

5.

6.

7.

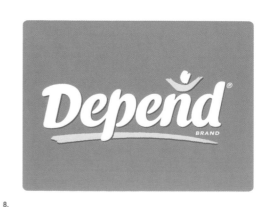

8.

9.

10.

11.

12.

 CELLEXPOWER™

13.

14.

15.

1, 2, 4, 5, 8, 10, 11, 14
Design Firm **Pedersen Gesk**
3, 7, 9
Design Firm **TGD Communications, Inc.**
6, 12, 13, 15
Design Firm **Karacters Design Group**

1.
Client   *Schwan's Sales Enterprises—Red Baron Brand*
Designers Rony Zibara, John Piper

2.
Client   *Schwan's Sales Enterprises—Schwan's Home Service Brand*
Designers Rony Zibara, Tracy Ghan

3.
Client   *FireBoxx, LLC*
Designer Gloria Vestal

4.
Client   *Tone Brothers—Tone's Brand*
Designers Rony Zibara, Beth Keys

5.
Client   *Tone Brothers—Durkee Brand*
Designers Rony Zibara, Beth Keys

6.
Client   *CC Beverage Company*
Designers Maria Kennedy, Matthew Clark

7.
Client   *Society of Cable Telecommunications Engineers*
Designer Gloria Vestal

8.
Client   *Kimberly Clark—Depend Brand*
Designers Rony Zibara, Scott Paul

9.
Client   *Association of Government Accountants*
Designers Chris Harrison, Jennifer Cedoz

10.
Client   *Schwan's Sales Enterprises—Tony's Brand*
Designers Rony Zibara, Scott Paul

11.
Client   *Clorox—STP Brand*
Designers Rony Zibara, John Piper

12.
Client   *Spintopia*
Designers Maria Kennedy, Roy White, Jeff Harrison

13.
Client   *Cellex*
Designers Maria Kennedy, Roy White, Nancy Wu

14.
Client   *Pactiv—Hefty Brand*
Designers Rony Zibara, John Piper

15.
Client   *CC Beverage Company*
Designers Maria Kennedy, Matthew Clark, Michelle Melenchuk

1.

2.

3.

4. PRODUCTIONS

FIFTH SET
INTERNATIONAL, INC

5.

EAGLE PASS CAMINO REAL INTERNATIONAL BRIDGE

6.

7.

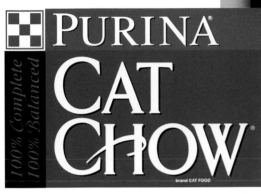

1.

2.

3.

Thoroughbred
Technologies

4.

STAND

Stress, anxiety and depression
affect one in four people.
Lack of understanding affects everyone.

5.

Set-Aside

6.

7.

see the sound

8.

THE IRON BED COMPANY

9.

10.

Women. Men. Different. Equal.
Equal Opportunities Commission

11.

MILITARY ASSISTANCE COMPANY

12.

Impact
Training Services, Inc.

13.

ELIZABETH FINN TRUST

14.

15.

1.

2.

3.

4.

5.

6.

7.

8

9.

10.

hooch&pooch

11.

12.

13.

14.

15.

1.

*Neuvo Latino
Restaurant & Night Club*

2.

THE PEER GROUP

PLASTIC SURGERY CENTER

For Men & Women

3.

N E X T

M E D I A

4.

PLUM

5.

UP

STEP

P R O J E C T

Advancement
Through
Education

6.

7.

maize

New American Cuisine

8.

9.

10.

11.

12.

13.

14.

15.

1 - 3, 6 - 10, 12, 13
Design Firm **PM Design**
4, 5, 11, 14, 15
Design Firm **Made On Earth**

1.
Client   *Babalu*
Designers   Philip Marzo, Andrei Koribanics

2.
Client   *B. Heaven*
Designer   Philip Marzo

3.
Client   *Peer Group*
Designer   Philip Marzo

4.
Client   *Next Media*
Designer   Jay Vigon

5.
Client   *Plum Productions*
Designer   Jay Vigon

6.
Client   *AY. PR.*
Designer   Philip Marzo

7.
Client   *24 by 7 Dating*
Designers   Philip Marzo, Andrei Koribanics

8.
Client   *Maize*
Designer   Russ Mowry

9.
Client   *South City Grill*
Designer   Philip Marzo

10.
Client   *Pomptonian Food Service*
Designers   Philip Marzo, Andrei Koribanics

11.
Client   *Post Logic Studios*
Designer   Jay Vigon

12.
Client   *Executive Solutions*
Designer   Philip Marzo

13.
Client   *B. Riccitelli Photography*
Designer   Philip Marzo

14.
Client   *Mohawk Productions*
Designer   Jay Vigon

15.
Client   *Necessary Evil*
Designer   Jay Vigon

1.

2.

EMPYREAN

3.

4.

ROCHESTER
RAMP PARK

5.

6.

big blue sky, inc.

7.

mercantec

8.

9.

10.

11.

12.

West Central Iowa
Solid Waste

Delivering Solid Waste Solutions...Together

13.

14.

15.

1.

2.

3.

LARRY'S CEDAR RIVER

SEAFOOD & OYSTER BAR

FRESH SEAFOOD

4.

Rēsendesign

5.

6.

7.

protegrity

8.

9.

10.

11.

12.

13.

General Atlantic Partners

14.

15.

1, 3, 4, 6, 7, 9 - 13
 Design Firm **DeLisle + Associates**
2, 5, 8, 14, 15
 Design Firm **Rēsendesign**
1.
 Client   Nico
 Designer Marty Csercsevits
2.
 Client   Intellego
 Designer Ken Resen
3.
 Client   Imagination Engineering
 Designer Tom DeLisle
4.
 Client   Larry's Cedar River
 Designer Tim DeLisle
5.
 Client   Rēsendesign Inc.
 Designers Ken Resen, Alison Mann
6.
 Client   Disney Cruise Line
 Designers Jack Crouse IV, Tim DeLisle
7.
 Client   Event Marketing & Mgmt. Int'l
 Designers Marty Csercsevits, Michael Ruge

8.
 Client   Protegrity, Incorporated
 Designer Ken Resen
9.
 Client   WDW Travel Industry Mktg.
 Designer Marty Csercsevits
10.
 Client   JacobDavis Productions
 Designer Marty Csercsevits
11.
 Client   Event Marketing & Mgmt. Int'l
 Designer Marty Csercsevits
12.
 Client   Cogistics, Inc.
 Designer Michael Ruge
13.
 Client   Church Street Entertainment
 Designer Tim DeLisle
14.
 Client   General Atlantic Partners
 Designer Ken Resen
15.
 Client   KM Management
 Designer Ken Resen

1.

2.

3.

GLOBAL

SERVICES

4.

NAS PATUXENT RIVER

OPERATIONAL ENVIRONMENTAL
PLANNING OFFICE

5.

6.

7.

8.

United States Australian Football League

SPRING 2001
ORLANDO
FLORIDA
MARCH 25-28

9.

WASHINGTON CAPITALS
ROAD CREW
CAPSROADCREW.COM

10.

STONEHAVEN

11.

SUPREMO

12.

13.

MAGIC YEARS
A RASHTi&RASHTi BABi GiFT

14.

The BuildingBox™

15.

1 - 6		
Design Firm	**Graves Fowler Associates**	
7		
Design Firm	**Mires**	
8		
Design Firm	**Clockwork Design**	
9, 10		
Design Firm	**McGaughy Design**	
11, 14		
Design Firm	**Muts & Joy & Inc.**	
12, 13		
Design Firm	**Mastandrea Design, Inc.**	
15		
Design Firm	**Nolin Branding & Design Inc.**	
1.		
Client	*United States Catholic Conference*	
Designer	Victoria Q. Robinson	
2.		
Client	*George Mason University*	
Designer	Elaine Chow	
3.		
Client	*Global Services*	
Designer	Esther Kang	
4.		
Client	*Camber Group*	
Designer	Esther Kang	
5.		
Client	*National Association of Attorneys General*	
Designer	Viviane Moritz	

6.		
Client	*Anchor Mental Health*	
Designer	Kenzie Raulin	
7.		
Client	*Exario*	
Designers	José Serrano, David Adey	
8.		
Client	*US Footy*	
Designer	Steve Gaines	
9.		
Client	*National Postal Forum*	
Designer	Malcolm McGaughy	
10.		
Client	*Washington Capitals Road Crew*	
11.		
Client	*Banfi Vintners*	
Designers	Akira Otani, Muts Yasumura	
12.		
Client	*Creagri*	
Designer	Mary Anne Mastandrea	
13.		
Client	*Mark Anthony Brands*	
Designer	Mary Anne Mastandrea	
14.		
Client	*Rashti & Rashti/Magic Years*	
Designers	Akira Otani, Joy Greene	
15.		
Client	*Reño—Dépôt*	
Designer	Gilles Legault	

1.

2.

james alan
SALON

3.

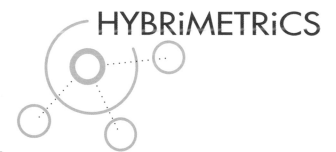

BARKLEY
D I S T R I C T

4.

HYBRiMETRiCS

5.

6.

dawson
CONSTRUCTION INC

7.

8.

mark
bergsma
G A L L E R Y

9.

WESTERN
ASSOCIATED STUDENTS
BOOKstore

10.

L I S A   E R S H I G   I N T E R I O R S

11.

**6iXTH
STREET**
WATERFRONT

PROPERTIES

12.

**PACIFIC
MARINE**
FOUNDATION

13.

B E L L I N G H A M
FESTIVAL *of* MUSIC

14.

TURNING POINT
realty advisors, LLC

15.

1.

2.

3.

4.

5.

6.

7.

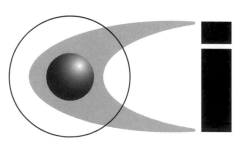

8.

9.

10.

11.

12.

13.

(all)

Design Firm **AKA Design, Inc.**

1.
Client   *The Center for*
          Transforming Worship
Designer Mike Mullen

2.
Client   *Ulysses S. Grant National*
          Historic Site—Jefferson National
          Parks Association
Designers John Ahearn, Richie Murphy

3.
Client   *Gateway Arch—Jefferson*
          National Parks Association
Designers John Ahearn, Richie Murphy

4.
Client   *MedEv LLC*
Designer Richie Murphy

5.
Client   *The Daily Perc*
Designer J.R. Gain

6.
Client   *Old Courthouse—Jefferson*
          National Parks Association
Designers John Ahearn, Richie Murphy

7.
Client   *City of Hazelwood*
Designer Craig Martin Simon

8.
Client   *Object Computing, Inc.*
Designer Mike Mullen

9.
Client   *Kirkwood/Webster YMCA*
Designer John Ahearn

10.
Client   *Recreation Station*
Designers Stacy Lanier, Craig Martin Simon

11.
Client   *102nd Annual Session—American*
          Association of Orthodontists
Designer Mike Mullen

12.
Client   *Illinois Special Olympics—*
          East Central Area 9
Designer Amy Ray

13.
Client   *AKA Design, Inc.—15th Anniversary*
Designer Richie Murphy

1.

3.

5.

7.

2.

4.

6.

1, 4, 5
Design Firm **Liquid Agency, Inc.**
2, 3, 6
Design Firm **The Focus Group**
7
Design Firm **DavisPartners**
1.
Client   *Private Label*
Designers   Alfredo Muccino, Jill Steinfeld,
            Robert Wong
2.
Client   *Loomis, Fargo, & Company*
Designer   Kirk Davis
3.
Client   *Loomis, Fargo, & Company*
Designer   Kirk Davis
4.
Client   *Private Label*
Designers   Alfredo Muccino, Jill Steinfeld,
            Robert Wong
5.
Client   *Private Label*
Designers   Alfredo Muccino, Jill Steinfeld,
            Robert Wong

6.
Client   *Loomis, Fargo, & Company*
Designer   Kirk Davis
7.
Client   *State Colleges of Massachusetts*
Designers   Tom Davis, Ken Cool
opposite
Design Firm **[i]e design, Los Angeles**
Client   *Cal Fed Bank, Aspen Program*
Designers   Marcie Carson, Cya Nelson

1.

The Power to Communicate.

2.

VERMONT LIVING AT **QUECHEE LAKES**

3.

UNIVERSITY of OREGON
SUMMER
S E S S I O N

4.

UNIVERSITY of OREGON
SUMMER
S E S S I O N

5.

BARRIER *flex* ™

6.

PERCEPTION
C O M M U N I C A T I O N S, I N C.

7.

UNIVERSITY of OREGON
SUMMER
S E S S I O N

8.

9.

10.

MetroMedia**Technologies**

IMAGING REDEFINED

11.

12.

GOLDSAND

13.

DaVita™

14.

THE POINTE
AT LEHI

15.

1, 9, 12, 13
Design Firm **Design North**
2, 7, 11, 14, 15
Design Firm **[i]e design, Los Angeles**
3, 6
Design Firm **DavisPartners**
4, 5, 8, 10
Design Firm **Funk & Associates**
1.
Client *Calm Air*
Designer Volker Beckmann
2.
Client *Media Pointe*
Designers Marcie Carson, Cya Nelson
3.
Client *Quechee Lakes*
Designers Tom Davis, Chuck Taylor
4.
Client *UO Summer Session*
Designer Beverly Soasey
5.
Client *UO Summer 2001-B*
Designer Beverly Soasey
6.
Client *Redington LLC*
Designers Tom Davis, Glenn Soulia

7.
Client *Perception Communications, Inc.*
Designers Marcie Carson, Amy Klass
8.
Client *UO Summer 2001-A*
Designer Beverly Soasey
9.
Client *Northwest Development Corporation*
Designer Volker Beckmann
10.
Client *Extraordinary Work Group*
Designer Beverly Soasey
11.
Client *Metromedia Technologies*
Designers Marcie Carson, Richard Haynie
12.
Client *Burntwood Hotel*
Designer Volker Beckmann
13.
Client *Goldsand Adventures*
Designer Volker Beckmann
14.
Client *Da Vita Inc.*
Designers Marcie Carson, Cya Nelson
15.
Client *Gilad Development*
Designers Marcie Carson, Cya Nelson

THOMPSON
Chiropractic
C·L·I·N·I·C

1.

2.

GEORGIA WORLD CONGRESS CENTER

THE Gift Fair
IN ATLANTA™

3.

Collegiate
Health Care

4.

early
INSURANCE

5.

annual color
exterior design

6.

Secret

7.

1, 5
Design Firm **Design North**
2
Design Firm **Logos Identity by Design Limited**
3, 6
Design Firm **cottrill design**
4
Design Firm **DavisPartners**
7
Design Firm **Fixgo Advertising (M) Sdn Bhd**
1.
Client   *Thompson Chiropractic Clinic*
Designer   Volker Beckmann
2.
Client   *TDP Inc.*
Designer   Gabriella Sousa
3.
Client   *urban expositions*
Designer   Allison Cottrill
4.
Client   *Collegiate Health Care*
Designers   Tom Davis, Ken Cool

5.
Client   *Early Insurance*
Designer   Volker Beckmann
6.
Client   *Annual Color*
Designer   Allison Cottrill
7.
Client   *Tohtonku Sdn Bhd*
Designer   FGA Creative Team
opposite
Design Firm **Mires**
Client   *The Yellow Pages*
Designers   Jose Serrano, Brian Fandetti,
           Miguel Perez

1.

2.

3.

4.

5.

6.

7.

8.

9.

10.

11.

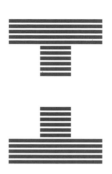

THE TORONTO HOSPITAL

12.

13.

14.

15.

BRUNO'S Since 1954 **WAX PEPPERS**

1.

Stanislaus County Library Foundation

2.

WARP & WOOF

A D V I S O R S

3.

ann loureiro p**ART**y **line**

4.

SALON SALON

5.

MICHAEL HAT FARMING

6.

P. Wexford's Pub

7.

SAMARITAN VILLAGE

8.

INTER-FAITH MINISTRIES

REACHING OUT TO THOSE IN NEED...

9.

Four Seasons Farms

10.

Marcia Herrmann Design

11.

AN INTERNET COFFEE BAR

12.

WristWand™

13.

HOTEL REX

SAN FRANCISCO

14.

i Horses

15.

1 - 14			**8.**	
Design Firm	**Marcia Herrmann Design**		Client	*Samaritan Village*
15			Designer	Marcia Herrmann
Design Firm	**Funk & Associates**		**9.**	
1.			Client	*Interfaith Ministries*
Client	*Brunos Peppers*		Designer	Marcia Herrmann
Designer	Marcia Herrmann		**10.**	
2.			Client	*Four Seasons Farms*
Client	*Stanislaus County Foundation*		Designer	Marcia Herrmann
Designer	Marcia Herrmann		**11.**	
3.			Client	*Marcia Herrmann Design*
Client	*Warp & Woof*		Designer	Marcia Herrmann
Designer	Marcia Herrmann		**12.**	
4.			Client	*Wired*
Client	*Ann Loureiro*		Designer	Marcia Herrmann
Designer	Marcia Herrmann		**13.**	
5.			Client	*Wristwand*
Client	*Salon Salon*		Designer	Marcia Herrmann
Designer	Marcia Herrmann		**14.**	
6.			Client	*Hotel Rex*
Client	*Michael Hat Farming*		Designer	Marcia Herrmann
Designer	Marcia Herrmann		**15.**	
7.			Client	*iHorses*
Client	*P. Wexfords Pub*		Designers	Beverly Soasey, Alex Wijnen
Designer	Marcia Herrmann			

1.

2.

3.

4.

5.

6.

7.

1
Design Firm **Spine Design**
2, 5, 6
Design Firm **Tieken Design &**
Creative Services
3, 4
Design Firm **Primo Angeli Inc.**
7
Design Firm **Julia Tam Design**
1.
Client   *Wizards Family Center*
Designer   Laurie Shattuck
2.
Client   *Lumature*
Designer   Rik Boberg
3.
Client   *MyRoad.com*
Designer   Toby Sudduth
4.
Client   *DevX*
Designer   Toby Sudduth
5.
Client   *Subway*
Designers   Fred E. Tieken, Lisette Sacks

6.
Client   *Subway*
Designers   Fred E. Tieken, Lisette Sacks
7.
Client   *Tao Tao*
Designer   Julia Chong Tam
opposite
Design Firm **The Douglas Group**
Client   *The Houston Astros' Enron Field*
Designers   Frank Douglas, Juliana Marek,
Duane Farthing
Photographer
Aker/Zvonkovic

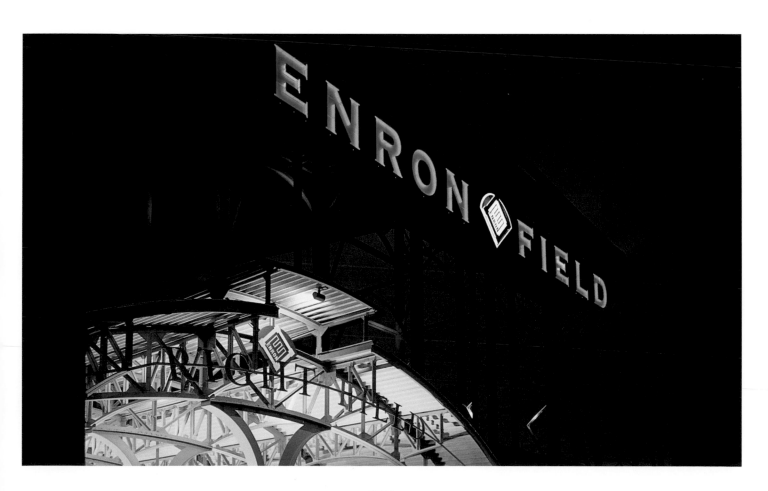

1.

2.

KOLTER

3.

4.

5.

6.

7.

8.

9.

TRELLIS

10.

agora

11.

TIPTOP
Since / Depuis
1909

12.

NEXUS

13.

14.

15.

1		
	Design Firm **Funk & Associates**	
2 - 15		
	Design Firm **Karo (Toronto) Inc.**	
1.		
	Client	*Garden Architecture*
	Designer	Alex Wijnen
2.		
	Client	*Sprint Canada*
	Designers	Michael Malloy, Shawn Rasmussen
3.		
	Client	*Kolter Developments*
	Designers	Paul Browning, Iwona Sowinski
4.		
	Client	*CryoCath Technologies Inc.*
	Designers	Paul Browning, Derek Wessinger, Shawn Rasmussen
5.		
	Client	*Sara Thompson Asso.*
	Designers	Paul Browning, Josie Sena
6.		
	Client	*Universe2U*
	Designers	Paul Browning, Paola Beltrame
7.		
	Client	*The Learning Alliance*
	Designers	Paul Browning, Iwona Sowinski

8.		
	Client	*Hospitals of Ontario Pension Plan*
	Designers	Michael Malloy, Joseph Chan, Steve Valentim
9.		
	Client	*City of Oakville*
	Designers	Paul Browning, Michael Malloy, Iwona Sowinski
10.		
	Client	*Trellis Corporation*
	Designers	Michael Malloy, Paola Beltrame
11.		
	Client	*Oshawa Food Group*
	Designers	Paul Browning, Peter Baker
12.		
	Client	*Tip Top Tailors*
	Designers	Michael Malloy, Maria Arshavsky
13.		
	Client	*Nexus Group International*
	Designers	Michael Malloy, Derwyn Goodall
14.		
	Client	*Polus Center*
	Designer	Mike Melnyk
15.		
	Client	*Humber College*
	Designers	Paul Browning, Nuno Ferreira, Derek Wessinger

1.

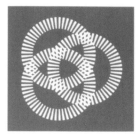

Greater Jamaica
Development
Corporation

2.

3.

ThemeMarks™

4.

5.

6.

7.

1, 3, 5, 7
Design Firm **Epstein Design Partners, Inc.**
2
Design Firm **Calori & Vanden-Eynden**
4, 6
Design Firm **Design North, Inc.**
1.
Client *Richland Development Corp.*
Designers Marla Gutzwiller, Jileen Coy
2.
Client *Greater Jamaica Dev. Corp*
Designers David Vanden-Eynden,
Marisa Schulman
3.
Client *Richland Development Corp.*
Designers Marla Gutzwiller, Jileen Coy
4.
Client *Fox River Paper Co.*
Designer Mark Topczewski
5.
Client *Richland Development Corp.*
Designers Marla Gutzwiller, Jileen Coy

6.
Client *Wellmark*
Designer Patrick Cowan
7.
Client *Richland Development Corp.*
Designers Marla Gutzwiller, Jileen Coy
opposite
Design Firm **Hornall Anderson Design Works**
Client *Grapefinds*
Designers Jack Anderson, Lisa Cerveny,
Mary Chin Hutchison,
Jana Wilson Esser, Gretchen Cook

PARK 5

1. BISTRO

intuıgy

2.

ClipperNet^{SM}
C O R P O R A T I O N

3.

CLOVIS
CALIFORNIA

4.

café
YUMM!

5.

Arlie & Company
LAND AND INVESTMENTS

6.

SANDWICHES · ESPRESSO · JUICES · TEAS
AVOLÁRE
SOUP · SALADS · MUFFINS · FRUIT · BAGELS

7.

Wings
BAR & GRILLE

8.

ShelterCare
Hope is here.

9.

UNIVERSITY
HOUSING
OF OREGON

10.

Chambers
P R O D U C T I O N S

11.

OTN

Oregon Transportation Network

12.

EUGENE PUBLIC LIBRARY FOUNDATION

13.

Summer Oaks
B U S I N E S S   P A R K

14.

DEQ

State of Oregon
**Department of
Environmental
Quality**

15.

(all)
Design Firm **Funk & Associates**

1.
Client	*Park 5 Bistro*
Designer	Beverly Soasey

2.
Client	*Intuigy*
Designer	Lada Korol

3.
Client	*Clippernet*
Designer	Beverly Soasey

4.
Client	*Clovis*
Designer	Chris Berner

5.
Client	*Café Yumm*
Designer	Chris Berner

6.
Client	*Arlie & Company*
Designer	Beverly Soasey

7.
Client	*Avolaré*
Designer	Chris Berner

8.
Client	*Wings Bar & Grille*
Designer	Chris Berner

9.
Client	*Sheltercare*
Designers	Alex Wijnen, Lada Korol

10.
Client	*UO Housing*
Designer	Beverly Soasey

11.
Client	*Chambers Production*
Designer	Kathleen Heinz

12.
Client	*Oregon Transportation Network*
Designer	Beverly Soasey

13.
Client	*Eugene Public Library Foundation*
Designers	Kathleen Heinz, Beverly Soasey

14.
Client	*Summer Oaks*
Designers	Chris Berner, Beverly Soasey

15.
Client	*DEQ*
Designers	Chris Berner, Beverly Soasey

1.

2.

3.

4.

5.

6.

7.

1
　Design Firm **Inca Tanvir Advertising Limited**
2, 7
　Design Firm **Meteor Creative**
3
　Design Firm **Bremmer & Goris
　　　　　　　Communications**
4, 5
　Design Firm **Design North, Inc.**
6
　Design Firm **Gregory Gersch**
1.
　Client　　　*Dubai Flying Association*
　Designer　　Suresh Pawar
2.
　Client　　　*Meteor Creative*
　Designers　 Daniel Conlan, Gregory Gersch
3.
　Client　　　*World Wildlife Fund International*
　Designer　　Gregory Gersch
4.
　Client　　　*Search Dog, Inc.*
　Designer　　Patrick Cowan

5.
　Client　　　*Car X Service Systems, Inc.*
　Designer　　Mark Topczewski
6.
　Client　　　*Frank Parsons Paper*
　Designer　　Gregory Gersch
7.
　Client　　　*EnterActing*
　Designers　 Gregory Gersch, Daniel Conlan
opposite
　Design Firm **Liquid Agency, Inc.**
　Client　　　*Liquid Agency, Inc.*
　Designers　 Alfredo Muccino, Joshua Swanbeck

1.

2.

3.

4.

EATFLEET

Harness the Power of One

5.

PLANET PROMOTIONS

"Just givin' it away"

6.

7.

8.

9.

10.

11.

ShopallAmerica.com™

12.

S2k

13.

Dream Dance

14.

The Northern Lights Theater
— AT POTAWATOMI BINGO CASINO —

15.

1.

2.

FISHER BUILDING

CITY APARTMENTS

3.

Collage

4.

MUSEUM OF NEW ART

5.

the world's best investors found here

marketocracy™

6.

7.

1
　　Design Firm **Studio 405**
2
　　Design Firm **Smarteam Communications Inc.**
3, 5
　　Design Firm **Skidmore, Inc.**
4, 6, 7
　　Design Firm **Studiomoon**
1.
　　Client　　　*AIGA Washington, DC Chapter*
　　Designers　Jodi Bloom, Jessica Snyder
2.
　　Client　　　*Information Technology*
　　　　　　　　Resellers Association
　　Designers　Gary Ridley, Brent Almond,
　　　　　　　　Sharisse Steber
3.
　　Client　　　*Village Green Companies*
　　Designers　Julie Pincus, Scott Olds
4.
　　Client　　　*Collage Lifestyle Salon*
　　Designer　　Tracy Moon

5.
　　Client　　　*Museum of New Art—MONA*
　　Designer　　John Latin
6.
　　Client　　　*Marketocracy*
　　Designer　　Tracy Moon
7.
　　Client　　　*Boogie Board*
　　Designer　　Tracy Moon
opposite
　　Design Firm **Studiomoon**
　　Client　　　*Lenox Restaurant*
　　Designers　Justine Descollonges, Tracy Moon

1.

2.

U P P E R C A S E

3.

VILLAGE
PARK

APARTMENTS

4.

carpe!centum

5.

ChicagoBroker.com

6.

ASH · MAISEY

D E N T I S T R Y

7.

SHADES OF LIGHT
STUDIO

8.

9.

FRIENDS ✶ OF
SIGNAL HILL
CULTURAL ARTS

10.

11.

12.

13.

14.

15.

1, 4
  Design Firm **Skidmore, Inc.**
2, 3, 6
  Design Firm **Pivot Design, Inc.**
5, 7
  Design Firm **Richards & Swensen**
8 - 15
  Design Firm **Simple Green Design**
1.
  Client   *Detroit Institute of Art*
  Designer   John Latin
2.
  Client   *Alzheimer's Association*
  Designer   Jennifer Stortz
3.
  Client   *Uppercase Books, Inc.*
  Designers Brock Haldeman, Liz Haldeman
4.
  Client   *Village Green Communities*
  Designer   Robert Nixon
5.
  Client   *Dunn Communication*
  Designer   William Swensen
6.
  Client   *ChicagoBroker.com*
  Designer   Don Emery

7.
  Client   *Dunn Communications*
  Designer   William Swensen
8.
  Client   *Shades of Light Studio*
  Designer   Wesley J. Su
9.
  Client   *Academy of Animation & Digital Art*
  Designer   Russ Scott
  Illustrator Norman Lao
10.
  Client   *Friends of Signal Hill Cultural Arts*
  Designer   Wesley J. Su
11.
  Client   *Simple Green*
  Designers Russ Scott, Mike Brower
12.
  Client   *Simple Green*
  Designers Russ Scott, Mike Brower
13.
  Client   *Natsume Koi Farm*
  Designer   Wesley J. Su
14.
  Client   *Bella Firma Pilates Studio*
  Designers Wesley Su, Mike Brower
15.
  Client   *R.O.C.K. Institute*
  Designers Mike Brower, Russ Scott
  Illustrators Norman Lao, Russ Scott

1.

2.

e st @ r t

3.

QI HE TANG

4.

INTERNATIONAL SPY MUSEUM

5.

PERKINS
SCHOOL FOR THE BLIND

6.

1
Design Firm **Rickabaugh Graphics**
2, 5, 6
Design Firm **Nesnadny + Schwartz**
3, 4
Design Firm **Ukulele Design
Consultants Pte Ltd**

1.
Client — *Morgan State University*
Designer — Dave Cap
2.
Client — *Crawford Museum of
Transportation and Industry*
Designers — Greg Oznowich,
Jennifer Hargreaves
3.
Client — *S & I Technologies Pte Ltd*
Designers — Kim Chun Wei, Lynn Lim
4.
Client — *Qi He Tang*
Designers — Verna Lim, Lynn Lim

5.
Client — *The International Spy Museum*
Designers — Tim Lachina, Greg Oznowich
6.
Client — *Perkins School for the Blind*
Designer — Greg Oznowich
opposite
Design Firm **Smith Design Associates**
Client — *Good Humor Breyers*
Designer — James C. Smith

1.

2.

3.

4.

5.

6.

7.

8.

9.

HAVANA CAY CIGAR BAR

10.

11.

Lighthouse Pointe

12.

Katy Mills

13.

MAGIC The Gathering PRO TOUR

14.

BEACH BAR

15.

1, 4, 5, 8, 14
Design Firm **Wizards of the Coast (In-House)**
2, 3, 7, 9 - 12, 15
Design Firm **ID8/RTKL Associates Inc.**
Client *Harbour Plaza*
Hotel Management Inc.

6, 13
Design Firm **ID8/RTKL Associates Inc.**
Client *The Mills Corporation*

1.
Client *Showdown Sports*
Designers Shauna Wolf-Narciso,
John Casebeer

2.
Designers Thom McKay, Jill Popowich,
John Scheffel, Jeff Wotoweic

3.
Designers Thom McKay, Jill Popowich

4.
Client *NFL Showdown Sports*
Designers Shauna Wolf-Narciso,
John Casebeer

5.
Client *NBA Showdown Sports*
Designers Shauna Wolf-Narciso,
John Casebeer

6.
Designers Charlie Greenawalt, Molly Miller,
Greg Rose, Jennifer Cardinal

7.
Designers Thom McKay, Jill Popowich

8.
Client *MLB Showdown Sports*
Designers Shauna Wolf-Narciso,
John Casebeer

9.
Designers Thom McKay, Keith Kellner,
John Scheffel, Jill Popowich

10.
Designers Thom McKay, Greg Rose

11.
Designers Thom McKay, Pornprapha
Phatanateacha, John Scheffel

12.
Designers Thom McKay, Jessica Koman

13.
Designers Charlie Greenawalt, Greg Rose,
Frank Christian

14.
Client *MTG Protour*
Designers Jeremy Bills, John Casebeer

15.
Designers Thom McKay, John Scheffel

1.

2.

3.

e.demartino design.

4.

5.

2001

SUMMER OUTING

6.

75 Years
RADIO CITY
ROCKETTES

7.

1.
Design Firm **Randi Wolf Design, Inc.**
Client   *Glassboro Center for the Arts—*
           Rowan University
Designers Randi Wolf, Amy Lebo, Mark Fields
2.
Design Firm **Chicoine Design + Illustration**
Client   *Chicoine Design + Illustration*
Designer   Roxane Chicoine
3.
Design Firm **Röka Inc.**
Client   *Chesapeake Capital Corporation*
Designer   Lizette Gecel
4.
Design Firm **E. DeMartino Design**
Client   *E. DeMartino Design*
Designer   Erick DeMartino
5.
Design Firm **Moscato Design**
Client   *Moscato Design*
Designer   Gerald Moscato

6.
Design Firm **E. DeMartino Design**
Client   *Sidley Austin Brown & Wood*
Designer   Erick DeMartino
7.
Design Firm **Hassenstein Design Inc.**
Client   *Radio City Entertainment*
Designer   Susanne Hassenstein
opposite
Design Firm **Smith Design Assoc.**
Client   *Hasbro, Inc.*
Designers Martha Gelber, Carol Konkowski

1.

2.

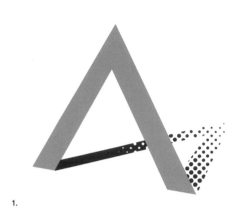

3.

4.

5.

6.

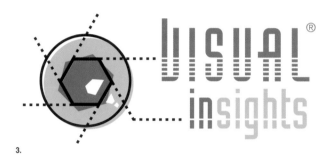

7.

8.

9.

10.

MANIFEST
INTERNATIONAL LLC
A Media Finance Consultancy

11.

WATER'S EDGE GARDENING
Wetscape Design

12.

13.

London's Internet Directory

14.

15.

1, 4, 7, 15
Design Firm **Smarteam Communications Inc.**
2, 3, 5, 8, 9, 13
Design Firm **StudioNorth**
6, 10 - 12, 14
Design Firm **Shields Design**

1.
Client · *Smarteam Communications Inc.*
Designers · Gary Ridley, Brent Almond
2.
Client · *The City of Lake Forest*
Designer · Laura Campbell
3.
Client · *Visual Insights*
Designer · Erik Peterson
4.
Client · *The Sugar Association*
Designers · Gary Ridley, Polina Pinchevsky
Illustrator · David Chen
5.
Client · *Equipment Central, Komatsu America International Company*
Designer · Mark Schneider
6.
Client · *Aquarius Aquarium*
Designer · Charles Shields

7.
Client · *Sutton Group*
Designers · Gary Ridley, Polina Pinchevsky
8.
Client · *Graver Outsourcing*
Designer · Misty Castaldi
9.
Client · *Deerpath Golf Course*
Designer · Steve Herberger
10.
Client · *maltwhiskey.com*
Designer · Charles Shields
11.
Client · *ManiFest International LLC*
Designer · Charles Shields
12.
Client · *Water's Edge Gardening*
Designer · Charles Shields
13.
Client · *Abbott Laboratories, Corporate Engineering Division*
Designer · Misty Castaldi
14.
Client · *NetLondon.com*
Designer · Charles Shields
15.
Client · *American Diabetes Association*
Designers · Gary Ridley, Brent Almond, Shariss Steber

1.

2.

CLEAN

3.

LAS ROSAS
COMPLEJO COMERCIAL

4.

THE PRINTWORKS

5.

ALGARVESHOPPING

6.

Bonaire
Parque Comercial y de Ocio

7.

1, 3
Design Firm **Motter-Design**

2
Design Firm **Source/Inc.**

4 - 7
Design Firm **RTKL—UK Ltd**

1.
Client   *Stiftung Maria Ebene*
Designers   Othmar Motter, Siegmund Motter

2.
Client   *Louis Kemp Seafood*

3.
Client   *Stiftung Maria Ebene*
Designers   Othmar Motter, Siegmund Motter

4.
Client   *Continente*
Designer   Glyn Rees

5.
Client   *Richardsons*
Designer   Glyn Rees

6.
Client   *Sonae Imobiliária*
Designer   Glyn Rees

7.
Client   *Grupo Riofisa*
Designer   Glyn Rees

opposite
Design Firm **Volan Design**
Client   *DataPlay*
Designer   Michele Braverman

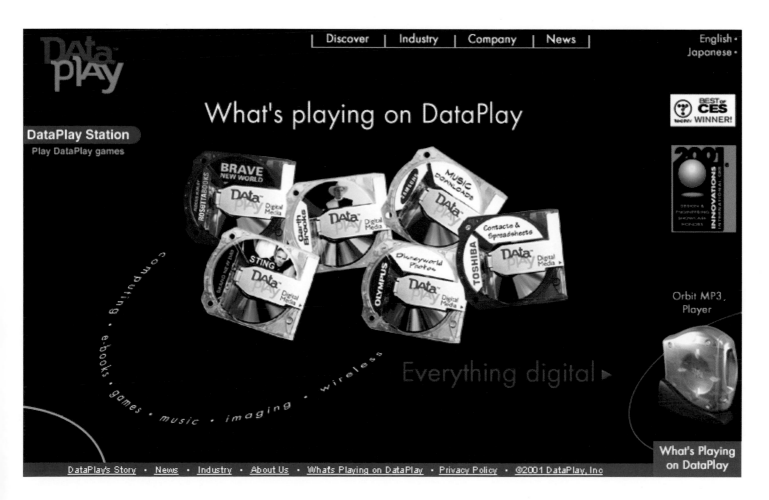

1.

2.

3.

4.

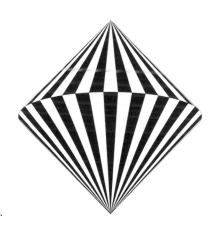

5.

6.

SENIOREN
BEIRAT

7.

8.

9.

10.

11.

12.

13.

14.

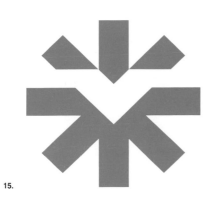

15.

(all)
Design Firm **Motter-Design**
1.
 Client   *Fellner-Fashion*
 Designer   Othmar Motter
2.
 Client   *Seepark Hard*
 Designer   Othmar Motter
3.
 Client   *Frick—Gartenbaubedarf, Vaduz*
 Designer   Othmar Motter
4.
 Client   *Die Stütze*
       (Jugendhilfswerk in Götzis, Austria)
 Designer   Othmar Motter
5.
 Client   *Spielwaren-Roth*
 Designers   Peter Motter, Othmar Motter
6.
 Client   *Dr. Hedwig Birnbaumer*
 Designers   Peter Motter, Othmar Motter
7.
 Client   *Senioren-Beirat*
       der Vorarlberger Landesregierung
 Designer   Othmar Motter

8.
 Client   *Österreichische Reitsport-Union*
 Designer   Othmar Motter
9.
 Client   *Mühlbauer, headwear*
       (Wien, Austria)
 Designer   Othmar Motter
10.
 Client   *Wasserkraftwerk Egg*
 Designer   Othmar Motter
11.
 Client   *Sportverein Salzbach*
 Designer   Othmar Motter
12.
 Client   *Bund Österreichischer Sportvereine*
 Designer   Othmar Motter
13.
 Client   *Austrian Embroideries*
 Designer   Othmar Motter
14.
 Client   *Internationaler Bodensee Club*
 Designer   Othmar Motter
15.
 Client   *Vorarlberger Handels-Zentrum AG*
 Designer   Othmar Motter

1.

Y O U T H
M U S E U M
E X H I B I T
COLLABORATIVE

2.

KISS IT GOODBYE!

3.

4.

madeirashopping

5.

6.

7.

1
Design Firm **Spark Design**
2 - 4, 7
Design Firm **The Douglas/Group**
5, 6
Design Firm **RTKL—UK Ltd**

1.
Client   *KnotKnown Records*
Designer   Rik Boberg

2.
Client   *Youth Museum Collaborative*
Designers   Dawn Diamond, James Wheat

3.
Client   *Disney's Anaheim Angels'*
            Kids Zone @ Edison Field
Designers   Juliana Marek, Dawn Diamond

4.
Client   *The Chattanoogan*
            Conference Center
Designers   Jim Alderman, Laura Wylie-McCoy

5.
Client   *Sonae Imobiliária*
Designer   Glyn Rees

6.
Client   *Société des Centres Commerciaux*
Designer   Glyn Rees

7.
Client   *Salt Lake City*
Designer   Dawn Diamond
opposite
Design Firm **Primo Angeli Inc.**
Client   *R. Torre & Company*
Designer   Toby Sudduth

1.

2.

3.

4.

5.

6.

7.

Seton Hall
University
School of Law

Seton Hall
University
School of Law
DEDICATED TO RIGOR
COMPASSION & SERVICE

8.

9.

10.

11.

12.

13.

(all)

Design Firm **Rickabaugh Graphics**

1.
Client Northern Illinois University
Designers Eric Rickabaugh, Dave Cap

2.
Client Dave & Buster's
Designer Eric Rickabaugh

3.
Client Atlas Color Imaging
Designer Eric Rickabaugh

4.
Client The Ohio State University
Designer Eric Rickabaugh

5.
Client The Ohio State University
Designer Eric Rickabaugh

6.
Client PAVE Advertising & Design/
Forsyth Furies
Designers Chris Bailey, Eric Rickabaugh

7.
Client 2 x 4 Studio/Coca-Cola/
Chicago Bears
Designer 2 x 4 Studio
Illustrator Jim Theodore

8.
Client Seton Hall University
Designer Eric Rickabaugh

9.
Client Huntington Banks
Designer Dave Cap

10.
Client City of Dublin
Designer Dave Cap

11.
Client Big East Conference
Designers Eric Rickabaugh, Dave Cap

12.
Client Royal Graphics
Designer Eric Rickabaugh

13.
Client Western Kentucky University
Designers Eric Rickabaugh, Dave Cap

1. [e]value

2. VAL VISTA MEADOWS

3. harter & associates

4. PRess Check

5. Leadership Café ™

6. CAPS RESEARCH

7. e-Touch SM

1 - 7
Design Firm **Spark Design**
1.
Client   *Avnet/Hallmark*
Designer Vince Adam
2.
Client   *Monterey Homes*
Designer Joe Gunsten
3.
Client   *Harter and Associates*
Designer Rik Boberg
4.
Client   *Avnet/Hallmark*
Designer Rik Boberg
5.
Client   *GSSC*
Designer Vince Adam
6.
Client   *Caps Research*
Designer Rik Boberg
7.
Client   *Avnet/Hallmark*
Designer Joe Gunsten

opposite
Design Firm **Smith Design Associates**
Client   *Parmalat—USA*
Designer Carol Konkowski

1
Design Firm **Spark Design**
2 - 7
Design Firm **Shook**
1.
Client   Aerial Wave
Designer   Joe Gunsten
2.
Client   Genuardi's Family Markets
Designers   Ginger Riley, Jeffrey Camillo
3.
Client   Bank of America
Designers   Ginger Riley, Jeffrey Camillo
4.
Client   Trillicom, LLC
Designers   Ginger Riley, Dave Gibson
5.
Client   SPOT'Z Gourmet Dogs &
               Frozen Custard
Designers   Ginger Riley, Jeffrey Camillo
6.
Client   Genuardi's Family Markets
Designers   Ginger Riley, Jeffrey Camillo

7.
Client   Genuardi's Family Markets
Designers   Ginger Riley, Jeffrey Camillo
opposite
Design Firm **Shook**
Client   Genuardi's Family Markets
Designers   Ginger Riley, Jeffrey Camillo

350

1.

2.

3.

BEVERLY

WINE CELLAR • CIGAR DIVAN • DISCOTHEQUE

4.

5.

6.

7.

8.

ItalianSpa

9.

10.

11.

Spring

12.

13.

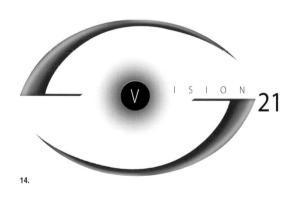

14.

15.

(all)

Design Firm **Ukulele Design Consultants Pte Ltd**

1.
Client   *The Diamond Place*
Designers   Kim Chun Wei, Mr. Chadir

2.
Client   *The Pan Pacific Hotel Singapore Pte Ltd*
Designers   Kim Chun Wei, Tee Siew Lin

3.
Client   *Prime Electrical Products (Pte) Ltd*
Designers   Kim Chun Wei, Lynn Lim

4.
Client   *Beverly*
Designers   Kim Chun Wei, Mr. Chadir

5.
Client   *Giesecke & Devrient Asia Pte Ltd*
Designers   Kim Chun Wei, Mr. Chadir

6.
Client   *Radiance Communications Pte Ltd*
Designers   Kim Chun Wei, Lee Shin Kee

7.
Client   *Ewis Aste Enterprise Pte Ltd*
Designers   Kim Chun Wei, Lynn Lim

8.
Client   *Prime Electrical Products (Pte) Ltd*
Designers   Kim Chun Wei, Lynn Lim

9.
Client   *Italian Spa*
Designers   Verna Lim, Lynn Lim

10.
Client   *Reed Exhibition Pte Ltd*
Designers   Kim Chun Wei, Lynn Lim

11.
Client   *IBM Singapore Pte Ltd*
Designers   Kim Chun Wei, Lee Shin Kee

12.
Client   *Prime Electrical Products (Pte) Ltd*
Designers   Kim Chun Wei, Lynn Lim

13.
Client   *Pretty Woman*
Designers   Verna Lim, Lynn Lim

14.
Client   *J.D. Edwards (Asia Pacific) Pte Ltd*
Designers   Kim Chun Wei, Lynn Lim

15.
Client   *e-Micro Corporation*
Designers   Kim Chun Wei, Stephanie Tan

1.

2.

3.

4.

5.

6.

7.

1, 4, 6
Design Firm **Fixgo Advertising (M) Sdn Bhd**
2, 3
Design Firm **Communication Via Design**
5, 7
Design Firm **EDAW Graphics Studio**

1.
Client *Omnisys dotcom*
Designers FGA Creative Team

2.
Client *Sedona Corporation*
Designers Victoria Adjami, Stephen Preston

3.
Client *Stonebridge Technology Associates*
Designers Victoria Adjami, Stephen Preston,
Cristine Corso

4.
Client *Cargosave*
Designers FGA Creative Team

5.
Client *EDAW, Inc.*
Designer Marty McGraw

6.
Client *Palmshine*
Designers FGA Creative Team

7.
Client *EDAW, Inc.*
Designer Marty McGraw

opposite
Design Firm **Hornall Anderson Design Works**
Client *Space Needle*
Designers Jack Anderson, Mary Hermes,
Gretchen Cook, Andrew Smith,
Julie Lock, Alan Florsheim,
Holly Craven, Elmer Dela Cruz,
Belinda Bowling, Amy Fawcette,
Tyler Cartier

space needle.

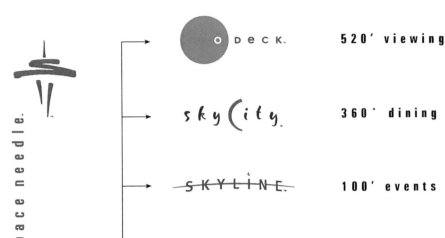

O DECK.   520' viewing

sky City.   360° dining

SKYLINE.   100' events

S·P·A·C·E.   100% shopping

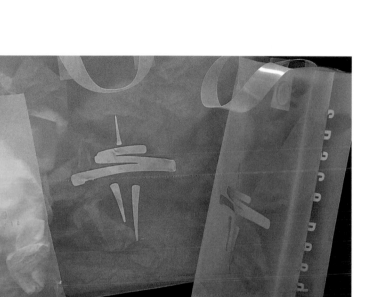

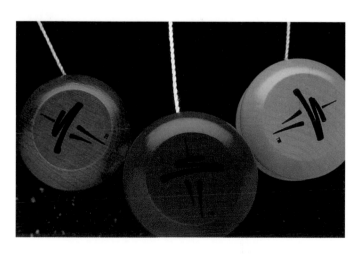

1.

2.

3.

4.

5.

6.

7.

8.

9.

10.

11.

12.

13.

STAFF BENEFITS SERVICES

14.

15.

1 - 13
Design Firm **Arista Advertising, Inc.**

14, 15
Design Firm **Ervin Bell Advertising**

1.
Client Towson Orthopetic Surgi Center
Designer Fanny Chakedis

2.
Client Baltimore Reads
Designers Fanny Chakedis, Rebecca Stevens

3.
Client International Elephant Foundation
Designers Fanny Chakedis, Pattie Gerding

4.
Client The Olson Group
Designers David Walper, Pattie Gerding

5.
Client McCormick + Company
Health Services
Designers David Walper, Rebecca Stevens

6.
Client McCormick + Company
Designer Fanny Chakedis

7.
Client Moore Sports Vision
Designers Fanny Chakedis, David Walper,
Patricia Gerding

8.
Client Mercy Medical Center
Designers Patricia Gerding, Fanny Chakedis

9.
Client Mercy Medical Center
Designer Patricia Gerding

10.
Client Moore Sports Vision
Designers Fanny Chakedis, David Walper,
Patricia Gerding

11.
Client Moore Sports Vision
Designers Fanny Chakedis, David Walper,
Patricia Gerding

12.
Client Mercy Medical Center
Designer Fanny Chakedis

13.
Client Cement Kiln Recycling Coalition
Designers David Walper, Fanny Chakedis

14.
Client SBS (Staff Benefits Services)
Designer Jileen Hohle

15.
Client HireCheck
Designer Jileen Hohle

1.

2.

3.

4.

5.

6.

7.

1 - 5
Design Firm **Iron Design**
6, 7
Design Firm **Blank, Inc.**

1.
Client   *AIDS Work of Tompkins County—Ride for Life 2001*
Designer   Louis Johnson

2.
Client   *Multi-City Technology Incubator*
Designers   Todd Edmonds, Jim Keller

3.
Client   *Thin Computing, Inc.—Betwin Software*
Designer   Jim Keller

4.
Client   *Avant Consulting*
Designer   Jim Keller

5.
Client   *Mimi Hockman*
Designer   Louis Johnson

6.
Client   *AssistMatch*
Designers   Danielle Weller, Robert Kent Wilson

7.
Client   *Coolspace*
Designers   Jason Thompson, Robert Kent Wilson

opposite
Design Firm **Desbrow & Associates**
Client   *Vocollect*
Designer   Brian Lee Campbell

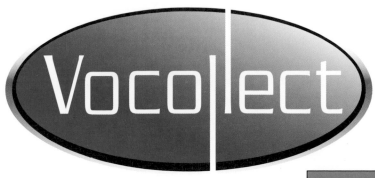

1.

2.

3.

4.

5.

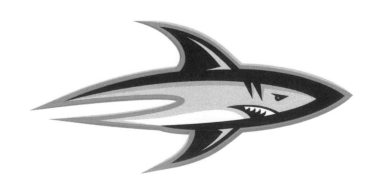

6.

7.

8.

9.

10.

RIDE FOR YOUTH

11.

12.

13.

14.

15.

(all)
Design Firm **Clockwork Design**
1 - 9, 11 - 13, 15
Designer Steve Gaines

1.
Client Sixman Football Association
Wolf Pack Team
2.
Client Sixman Football Association
3.
Client Spring Creek Animal Hospital
4.
Client Sixman Football Association
Raiders Football Team
5.
Client Sixman Football Association
Mad Dogs Football Team
6.
Client Precision Decks
7.
Client Puttnik Golf

8.
Client Sixman Football Association
Sharks Football Team
9.
Client Sixman Football Association
Rhinos Football Team
10.
Client South Texas
Golf Tournament Association
Designer Brian Badillo
11.
Client San Antonio North Central
Rotary Club
12.
Client Creative Club of San Antonio
13.
Client San Antonio Diablos
14.
Client The Psychological Corporation
Designer Jordan Merson
15.
Client Randolph Brooks
Services Group, LLC

**Quality
Vision
Services**

1.

2.

A Fielder Group Enterprise

3.

GLFEA

4.

[McELFISH + COMPANY]

5.

6.

MICROPURE

Water Services

7.

1, 2, 6
Design Firm **McElveney & Palozzi Design Group**

3 - 5, 7
Design Firm **McElfish + Company**

1.
Client *Optical Gaging Products (QVS)*
Designers Lisa Williamson, Matt Nowicki

2.
Client *Highfalls Brewing Company—Michael Shea's*
Designers Jon Westfall, Mike Johnson

3.
Client *Betz Trucking*
Designer Paul Aiuto

4.
Client *Great Lakes Fabricators & Erectors Association (GLFEA)*
Designer Paul Aiuto

5.
Client *McElfish + Company*
Designer Paul Aiuto

6.
Client *Legacy Construction Corporation*
Designers Jon Westfall, Matt Dundon

7.
Client *Micropure Water Services*
Designer Paul Aiuto

opposite
Design Firm **Hornall Anderson Design Works**
Client *Ghirardelli Chocolate Company*
Designers Jack Anderson, Debra McCloskey, Darlin Gray, Jana Wilson Esser, John Anderle, Mary Chin Hutchison, Beckon Wyld, Tobi Brown, Taro Sakita, Dorothee Soechting

CRC

1

PANE ITALIA PTE LTD

2.

D B & B

3.

heaven's **touch**

4.

MUMS & BABES

5.

嘉香大酒樓

KIA HIANG
restaurant

6.

the
jeunes
shop

7.

Water Ventures

8.

FAMILYCLICK

9.

THE
ATRIUM
LOUNGE

10.

UKULELE
DESIGN

11.

AROMAZ BAKERY & DELI

12.

Q doz

quintessential living

13.

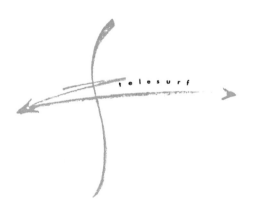

telesurf

14.

15.

1 - 8, 10 - 15
Design Firm **Ukulele Design Consultants Pte Ltd**

9
Design Firm **Muts & Joy & Inc.**

1.
Client   *Hewlett-Packard Singapore Pte Ltd*
Designers   Kim Chun Wei, Stephanie Tan

2.
Client   *Pane Italia*
Designers   Kim Chun Wei, Sim Choon Tee

3.
Client   *DB&B Pte Ltd*
Designers   Kim Chun Wei, Lee Shin Kee

4.
Client   *Heaven's Touch*
Designers   Kim Chun Wei, Lynn Lim

5.
Client   *Mums & Babes*
Designers   Kim Chun Wei, Stephanie Tan

6.
Client   *Kia Hiang Gourmet Pte Ltd*
Designers   Kim Chun Wei, Lynn Lim

7.
Client   *The Jeunes Shop*
Designers   Kim Chun Wei, Lee Shin Kee

8.
Client   *Water Ventures*
Designers   Kim Chun Wei, Tee Siew Lin

9.
Client   *FamilyClick.com*
Designers   Akira Otani, Muts Yasumura

10.
Client   *The Pan Pacific Hotel Singapore Pte Ltd*
Designers   Kim Chun Wei, Sim Choon Tee

11.
Client   *Ukulele Design Consultants Pte Ltd*
Designer   Verna Lim

12.
Client   *The Pan Pacific Hotel Singapore Pte Ltd*
Designer   Kim Chun Wei

13.
Client   *Qdoz*
Designers   Kim Chun Wei, Lynn Lim

14.
Client   *Telesurf*
Designers   Kim Chun Wei, Tee Siew Lin

15.
Client   *Yeo Hiap Seng Limited*
Designers   Kim Chun Wei, Stephanie Tan

P O L A R I S

1.

2.

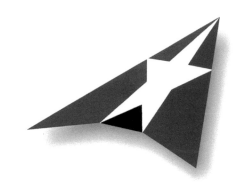

3.

ASSET | TRADE ™

4.

LaQuatra Bonci Associates

5.

PITTSBURGH SYMPHONY

6.

PITTSBURGH SYMPHONY
BRIDGES
Education & Community Outreach

7.

1, 2, 4
Design Firm **Orbit Integrated**
3
Design Firm **Michael Lee Advertising & Design, Inc.**
5 - 7
Design Firm **Agnew Moyer Smith**

1.
Client — *Polaris Consulting*
Designer — Heather Meakin

2.
Client — *Onexstream*
Designer — Orbit Integrated

3.
Client — *Southeast Texas Regional Airport*
Designer — Michael Lee

4.
Client — *AssetTrade*
Designer — Ed Abbott

5.
Client — *La Quatra Bonci Associates*
Designers — John Sotirakis, Lisa Vitalbo

6.
Client — *Pittsburgh Symphony*
Designer — John Sotirakis

7.
Client — *Pittsburgh Symphony*
Designer — John Sotirakis

opposite
Design Firm **Hornall Anderson Design Works**
Client — *XOW!*
Designers — Jack Anderson, Lisa Cerveny, Bruce Branson-Meyer, Mary Chin Hutchison, Jana Nishi, Don Stayner

1.

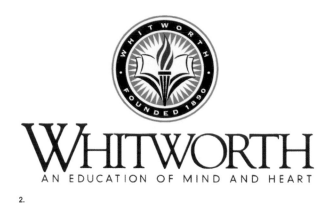

2.

3.

4.

5.

6.

7.

8.

ProManage
EXPERTS. INVESTING FOR YOU.

9.

NORTHWEST
MUSEUM
OF ARTS
& CULTURE

10.

SPOKANE PARKS
FOUNDATION

11.

Maryhill
WINERY

12.

13.

14.

The Human Potential Project

15.

(all)
Design Firm **Klündt Hosmer Design**
Designer Darin Klündt

1.
Client *Jacob's Java*
Designer Brian Gage

2.
Client *Whitworth College*
Designer Brian Gage

3.
Client *Mead School District*
Designer Lorri Feenan

4.
Client *Enerphaze*
Designers Eric Grinstead, Judy Heggem-Davis

5.
Client *Express Theatre Northwest*
Designer Lorri Feenan

6.
Client *Alera Lighting*
Designer Henry Ortega

7.
Client *Discovery School*
Designers Rick Hosmer, Lorri Feenan

8.
Client *Damon & Magnuson*
Designer Diane Mahan

9.
Client *ProManage*
Designer Henry Ortega

10.
Client *Northwest Museum of
Arts and Culture*
Designers Lorri Feenan, Brian Gage

11.
Client *Spokane Parks Foundation*
Designer Judy Heggem-Davis

12.
Client *Maryhill Winery*
Designer Judy Heggem-Davis

13.
Client *Webprint*
Designer Brian Gage

14.
Client *Fort Spokane Brewery*
Designers Judy Heggem-Davis, Eric Grinstead

15.
Client *The Human Potential Project*
Designer Lorri Feenan

1.

alternative
treatment

2.

BRITTEX
appraisal services, inc

3.

MUELLER

4.

SHELLY
DEVELOPMENT
CORPORATION

5.

HACKETT'S
Lawn Maintenance

6.

s○ckeye

NETWORKS

7.

1 - 6

Design Firm **Mark Spector, Architect**
Designer Mark Spector

7

Design Firm **Stewart Monderer**

1.
Client *Miami PC*

2.
Client *Alternative Treatment*

3.
Client *Brittex*

4.
Client *Mueller and Associates*

5.
Client *Shelly Development Corp.*

6.
Client *Hackett's*

7.
Client *Sockeye Networks, Inc.*
Designers Jeffrey Gobin, Stewart Monderer

opposite
Design Firm **Muts & Joy & Inc.**
Client *Banfi Vintners (Concha y Toro)*
Designers Tom Delaney, Akira Otani,
Gisele Sangiovanni

EST. 1883
CONCHA y TORO

1.

2.

3.

4.

5.

6.

7.

8.

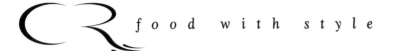 food with style

9.

10.

11.

Changing Lives. Every Day.

12.

digital **i**nteractive **g**roup

13.

14.

15.

1, 4 - 9, 11, 14, 15			**8.**		
Design Firm	**Watts Design**			Client	*Healesville Sanctuary*
2, 3, 10, 12, 13				Designer	Linda Ho
Design Firm	**Hansen Design Company**		**9.**		
Designers	Pat Hansen, Jacqueline Smith			Client	*Carol Rieley*
1.				Designer	David Fry
Client	*Beechwood Wines*		**10.**		
Designer	Peter Watts			Client	*Gibbons Lane Winery*
2.			**11.**		
Client	*Gardening Getaways*			Client	*Amway Australia*
3.				Designer	Helen Watts
Client	*True Martial Arts*		**12.**		
4.				Client	*Family Services*
Client	*Printing Industry Golfing Society*		**13.**		
Designer	Peter Watts			Client	*Digital Interactive Group*
5.			**14.**		
Client	*Swinburne University Hospital*			Client	*Darriwill Farm*
Designers	Peter Watts, Helen Watts			Designer	Peter Watts
6.			**15.**		
Client	*Span Communication*			Client	*World Amateur Putting Challenge*
Designer	David Fry			Designer	Peter Watts
7.					
Client	*Blackwood Studios*				
Designer	Peter Watts				

1.

2.

3.

4.

5.

6.

7.

1 - 7
Design Firm **Mark Spector, Architect**
Designer   Mark Spector
1.
Client   *Copperwood*
2.
Client   *Barstools and More*
3.
Client   *Rosi Vergara*
4.
Client   *Jonida International*
5.
Client   *Shelly Katz*
6.
Client   *Logan Lilly*
7.
Client   *Spector Builders*

opposite
Design Firm **Orbit Integrated**
Client   *Jack Harris*
Designer   Mark Miller

722 Yorklyn Road
Suite 150, Hockessin, DE 19707

v 302-477-1689 | 1-888-241-3103
f 302-477-1684

e jack.harris@jackharris.com
i www.jackharris.com

722 Yorklyn Road
Suite 150, Hockessin, DE 19707

v 302-477-1689 | 1-888-241-3103
f 302-477-1684

e jack.harris@jackharris.com
i www.jackharris.com

1.

Saint Peter Claver Church
A DIVERSE SPIRITUAL
COMMUNITY IN ACTION

2.

WineValet

3.

4.

5.

market
JAZZ

Buy, sell and all that jazz

6.

sky river ℠
How Broadband Flows

7.

STARLIGHT
THEATRE

8.

TIMESHARE SOURCE

9.

10.

SAN DIEGO WTC

11.

LIBERTY STATION

12.

13.

e stockoptions
Expertise for growth.℠

14.

CALIFORNIA
BENTO
QUICK HEALTHY FOOD

15.

1.

2.

3.

4.

5.

6.

LYNOTT & ASSOCIATES

7.

1, 2, 5
Design Firm **Phil Meilinger**
3, 4, 6, 7
Design Firm **Pollman Marketing Arts, Inc.**
1.
Client   *Blue Ridge Lawn & Garden*
2.
Client   *Cristo Rey Jesuit High School*
3.
Client   *Association Partners Plus*
Designers   Jennifer Pollman, Erin Trice
4.
Client   *Center for Executive Leadership*
Designers   Jennifer Pollman, Erin Trice
5.
Client   *Blue Frog Beads*
6.
Client   *Lynott & Associates*
Designers   Jennifer Pollman, Erin Trice
7.
Client   *Dayton Land and Real Estate*
Designers   Jennifer Pollman, Erin Trice

opposite
Design Firm **Hornall Anderson Design Works**
Client   *Widmer Brothers*
Designers   Jack Anderson, Larry Anderson,
                   Bruce Stigler, Bruce Branson-Meyer,
                   Mary Chin Hutchison, Kaye Farmer,
                   Ed Lee, Michael Brugman

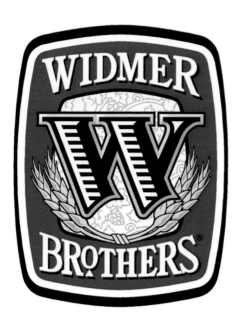

INDEX
Design Firms

Clients

383

384